THE NORTHERN GARDENER'S LIBRARY

Flower Gardens

Published by Linden Hills Press (a division of the Hohman Group, Inc.)

Trade distribution by Voyageur Press
P.O. Box 338
Stillwater, MN 55082

Page Layout and Assembly by Great Way Communications
Printed and bound in the United States by
Anderberg-Lund Printing Company

ISBN 0-9628378-1-4

Acknowledgements

The publisher is grateful to the following persons for making this book a reality. Dorothy Johnson for seeing the possibility. Jack Anderberg for his faith in us. Jodi Lind-Hohman of ARTGARDEN for her keen eye in selecting photos and for sharing her horticultural knowledge. The people at Great Way Communications for being able to follow my sometimes cryptic instructions. All the contributors to the Minnesota Horticulturist for their love of gardening and the ability and desire to share their many talents with the rest of us.

Thank you,
David Hohman
Publisher

Table of Contents

Chapter 1: Getting Started

Chapter 2: Perennials

Chapter 3: Annuals

Chapter 4: Bulbs

Chapter 5: Roses

Chapter 6: Appendices

Foreword

The Northern Gardener's Library is based upon articles originally published in *Minnesota Horticulturist* magazine. Trusted as a reliable resource to northern horticulture for more than 100 years, *Minnesota Horticulturist* is the oldest continuously-published periodical in Minnesota. The official publication of the Minnesota State Horticultural Society, *Minnesota Horticulturist* began by relating experiences of horticulturists who moved to Minnesota to help feed the growing population. These pioneers faced unexpected challenges, attempting to grow the fruits and vegetables they brought from Europe and the Eastern United States.

Minnesota Horticulturist has evolved to meet the needs of amateur horticulturists — gardeners who enjoy their hobby within small or large home grounds. Writers share their own experiences, which bring research and experimentation to a practical level in the home garden.

This book shares the experience of seasoned gardeners, many of whom write regularly for *Minnesota Horticulturist*. Their practical advice is based upon observations, trials and successes. Care has been taken to explain environmentally-conscious techniques and growing practices.

The first two volumes in The Northern Gardener's Library are being published in 1991: *The Good Gardener* and *Flower Gardens*. Future volumes will feature other popular horticultural themes.

All of the volumes in the series concentrate on the unique needs and challenges of growing home gardens in the lovely, but often harsh, climates of the Upper Midwest. Written for hardiness zones 3 and 4, the information on culture and varieties is also valuable for zone 5 gardens.

Introduction

Northern gardeners face a double whammy in short growing seasons and cold winters. Horticultural research and growers' experience have assisted home gardeners in growing beautiful, permanent flower gardens, with dazzling arrays of hardy perennials and bulbs, sun-loving annuals, and beautiful roses.

Flower Gardens shares the advice of home gardeners who have grown and enjoyed the plants they describe. The authors of this book are gardeners first and foremost and they write for people like themselves — for people like you. They offer their experience, their opinions, their encouragement, and most of all, their love of the art of the garden.

Living in the northern part of the United States no longer means having to grow only tundra plants, and look longingly at the bountiful, blooming plants of the southern and English gardens. This is the only book that makes our climate — and the rugged individuals who live in it — more than a footnote.

Both novice and experienced gardeners will enjoy the down-to-earth information. Readers will be inspired by the full-color photographs. A sampling of these pages will show you how to plan for perennial blooming times, experiment with some unusual bulbs, and tell you everything you ever wanted to know about roses (but were afraid to ask!)

Whether you curl up with it in front of a January fire in the fireplace, or take it into the garden when you're transplanting your first rose bush, it's a book you'll use for years to come.

> Dorothy Johnson
> Executive Director
> Minnesota Horticultural Society

P.S. The focus of this book is flowers, and while many of the articles contain culture and growing techniques, there was simply not enough room to include all the information that goes into a good garden. For basic information on such things as seed starting and propagation, garden care and other topics, refer to *The Good Gardener*, another volume in the series. Future volumes will contain additional information on particular plant varieties, specialty gardens, vegetables, and more.

Chapter 1

Getting Started

Be Your Own Landscape
Designer

A Basketful of Spring Tasks

Ingredients for Fabulous
Flowers

Be Your Own Landscape Designer

Fred Glasoe

Whether you're a first-time gardener, or an old hand like me, spring always presents the possibility of starting a new flower garden. Ask yourself what you can do differently this time around — or if it's your first garden, look around and learn from some of your friends and neighbors mistakes. Let's look at whether our gardens have gotten to be too much of a yearly routine. What can we do that's different and exciting?

The first new idea to consider is developing more interesting designs to replace the old rectangular flower bed pressed up against the fence or wall. Curved lines and round shapes seem to be nature's best artistic offering. I've never known a true "green thumber" who didn't dig out into the yard a little more each year, jamming in a few new varieties that just wouldn't fit into the already crowded flower bed.

Be your own landscape designer, and remodel your most boring garden shapes. Using a few in-and-out sweeps and curves, dip in and project out into the yard. Accent these new shapes with a few shapely bermed or raised beds right in the center of the yard, which will be reserved for roses, irises, mixed annuals or any other special hobby plantings.

Don't be overly concerned about how many little turns the lawn mower will have to make. Vegetable gardens can be very impressive with straight, neat edges and nice straight rows of crops, but flower gardens need curves that weave in and out, clusters and drifts of color, and varying plant heights. Get rid of straight, horizontal lines of plants that are all tall in the background, medium height in the middle, and short little rows along the front edge.

Break up horizontal and vertical lines with clumps of diagonal and oval plantings of all one variety. Sweeping one color in a direction that contrasts with another color creates a stunning effect. A flowering shrub, peony bush, or low-growing evergreen can help accent the contrasting heights and shapes of smaller plants. Boulders, sundials, and fountains can create special effects. Just don't go overboard and end up with an outside gallery of flamingos, paddle ducks, and the seven dwarfs.

Color is the raison d'etre of the flower garden. Showy perennials which bloom well are the backbone of a garden. Open spaces among the showoffs can be reserved for spring bulbs, and later filled in with the bright color of a favorite annual.

Since the grocery cart was introduced to the garden store, too many shoppers push up and down the aisles, picking up one box of everything and not enough of any one thing. This diminishes the effect of a well-planned collection. Planting one plant here and one plant there leaves you with a garden mishmash and the effect of color is lost. Purchase a few varieties in quantity, and plant each variety in a patch so that its color will hit the viewer's eye with a splash!

Last but not least, don't overdo. New gardeners can easily fade away on their first try if they take on too much or if they try to do it all in May. Gardening is a hobby to enjoy. If you can't enjoy, don't garden. On an early morning in late May, when it's quiet and still, when the air is light and fresh, when birds sing and new leaves rustle in the trees, take time to survey those new plants that you will nurture. Take time to enjoy your garden. Sniff the air. Feel the breeze on your face. Absorb the warmth of the spring sun. Good gardening!

Clusters and drifts of color will hit the viewer's eye with a splash! (Ben Gowen)

A Basketful of Spring Tasks

Fred Glasoe

Spring finds the gardener with a basket of tasks which he completes one by one, as time and weather permit, until the basket is empty. Neglect of any of them can result in horticultural failure. Some folks think that nothing can be done until the last May frost has left the area. Others, equally mistaken, get their timetable mixed up and try to plant tender annuals and perennials in mid-April. The calendar confusion muddles the grower's mind, but that is nothing compared to the confusion it creates in the growing plants. Sit down early in the spring and create your list of projects to fill your task basket. Here are some ideas, in case your basket seems a little empty.

(1) Remove leaves and cover from perennials as soon as the cover is soft and moveable. This is especially important for chrysanthemums and delphiniums which are easily suffocated. Rake out shrubbery, gardens, and building corners. Do not rake lawns with pull rakes until they are dry and firm.

(2) Medium and large-sized flower seeds can still be started indoors in early April. Be sure to use sterilized potting soil or sterile growing media. It's too late for tiny seeds like petunias and snapdragons, so plan to purchase plants in mid-May at your local greenhouse. The only seeds I start directly in my garden are zinnias, which do not enjoy being moved. They pop up in warm June soil in only a few days.

(3) If you didn't grow your own seedlings under lights this year, you will be making a trip to your local greenhouse or garden store. This can add up in cost, but it is much better than waiting for frost-free weather, thinking you are going to have a maze of bloom in your garden from seeds that were planted in mid-May. Most flower seeds need 8 to 12 weeks of growth just to be ready for transplanting, and if you wait until mid-May to plant seeds, you may find your peak bloom period occurring around September 1.

(4) April is too early to do much cultivation in perennial beds, so wait for feeding and planting until you can see what is growing where. Cover must be removed from any bulb-growing areas as soon as growth begins. If you are negligent about this, you'll lose a few tulip tops and spring flowers when you rake the garden beds.

(5) Don't till or turn over wet soil. This can cause you weeks of trouble with compacted soil and a loss of capillary action in the hot weeks ahead. Wait until the soil is partially dry, usually not until May.

(6) When the soil is ready to be worked, adding old, well-decomposed compost is always appropriate. A small amount of fertilizer can also be added, but before planting allow it to break down for a few days after mixing it into the soil to a depth of 8 to 12 inches. A loose, friable soil 12 to 15 inches deep is essential. Soil is at least 60 percent of your gardening success. Organic, well-drained soil with a near neutral pH of 6.7 to 7.2 is what you want.

(7) If you have failed to take up compost-making as a hobby, you're probably spending too much money on baled peat moss and overpriced bags of dehydrated cow or sheep manure. This organic material is beneficial to the soil, but to achieve adequate improvement, you may need several dozen bags. Learn to make compost and use your product for mulching, as well as for soil improvement.

(8) If you have partially rotted compost that is thawed out by mid-April, you can sprinkle it liberally with nitrogen (urea) and turn it. To start the decomposition as soon as possible, be sure you work it over so that it is loose and well ventilated. It can be ready for your late garden planting in May if you can get it to generate enough heat.

(9) Buried roses can usually be uncovered in mid-April in zone 4. I usually take my roses up between April 15-20. If you wait too long, the stems often bud out under the soil, and the new growth is broken up when the branches are lifted.

(10) Pick a nice warm day and clean out the garage or garden shed. If yours looks anything like mine (for your sake, I hope it doesn't), you will need this extra spring search period to find your fork and shovel and see if the hose is under the fall and winter oddments collection. I'm always looking for the hose nozzles and hand trowel. Each fall I try to remember to put these very small items in a special place so they won't get lost.

Ingredients For Great Gardens

Fred Glasoe

Watering

Water keeps plants growing by allowing roots to take up food. Soil that has been well prepared and mulched will need little watering except during dry spells. Don't wait until plants are severely wilted to water. Putting them under such stress causes them to sulk at the expense of bloom.

Water thoroughly. When dry, water once a week and apply one inch of water at a time. Frequent light watering encourages roots to grow near the soil surface, making the plant more susceptible to drought. The best way to water is with a soil soaker or a bubbler. With these methods there is very little evaporation or run-off, and the water seeps deep into the soil. Deep watering encourages deep rooting, and plants with well-formed root systems can withstand dry periods better. Remember also that the type of plant will determine the need for water. Shallow-rooted plants will need more frequent watering than deep-rooted plants.

If using overhead watering, water early in the day so that the foliage will dry quickly. Foliage that goes into the evening wet is especially vulnerable to fungus diseases, such as mildew.

Fertilizer

Fertilizer contains the elements which promote growth in our plants. It's important to know which plant parts these minerals support. Most garden fertilizers consist of 30 to 40 percent useable elements and 60 to 70 percent neutral filler. The working elements in fertilizers are nitrogen, phosphorous, and potassium. These are indicated by the percentage number on the container, such as 20-10-10. Some secondary elements such as iron, magnesium, calcium, sulphur, copper, zinc, or boron are often included.

Nitrogen, the first number in the analysis, keeps plants green and stimulates the growth of foliage. It is an excellent soil addition for such vegetables as lettuce, cabbage, chard, kale, and spinach. Dark green lawns and shade trees benefit greatly from high-nitrogen fertilizers. Both indoor and outdoor foliage plants find nitrogen a treat.

Look for a high second number if color or fruit production is what you desire. It indicates the phosphorous percentage. Phosphorous also stimulates root growth in new plants and root crops.

Potassium, represented by the third number, joins together as a catalyst with phosphorous, to ensure good metabolism, transpiration, and respiration in the plant. It also helps ensure hardiness and disease resistance.

We hear so much about organic and inorganic fertilizers. Both contain the elements that the plant world needs, but these elements are present in very different amounts and forms. Organic fertilizers come from plant and animal tissue and waste. They are slow acting and not always balanced in the way in which they meet nutritional needs. They seldom burn stems and roots if they are directly applied, and they are good for soil building and conditioning.

Inorganic fertilizers are mined minerals or laboratory chemical compounds that are water soluble. The nutrients are released quickly and can damage plants if the fertilizer is not properly diluted. Although they are fast acting and efficient, they do nothing to build up a good bulky, aerated soil, and should be used as a supplement to a good soil composting program.

Soil

Good garden soil should feel loose and crumble easily when squeezed. Most garden plants will not survive in poorly drained soil, such as the heavy clay-type soils which predominate in parts of the northern states. (Clay soil is easily identified. When wet, a handful of soil will hold together and feel sticky when squeezed. When dry, clay soils tend to become hard and cracked.) In some places, sandy soil prevails. (Sand cannot hold moisture, and nutrients are washed away from plant roots with constant watering.) Both clay and sandy soils need additions to become desirable growing media.

Sand added to clay or clay added to sand can improve overall soil composition. But the desired loam soil also contains organic matter. Compost, peat moss, decomposed farmyard manure, leaf mold, and grass clippings are the most important soil amendments for any soil type. Such organic matter will not only improve soil drainage, but will also promote aeration, reduce erosion, and supply plants with nutrients and micro-organisms which might otherwise be unavailable for plant use. Organic materials will also help to improve the general physical condition of the soil and aid in warming up the soil early in the spring.

To add organic materials, simply spread a two to three-inch layer

This annual bed looks fresh and healthy due to adequate water, good soil, a cooling mulch and the right fertilizer mix. (MSHS)

over the surface of the garden. Thoroughly mix this layer into the existing soil by spading or roto-tilling. Barnyard manure should be well composted (not fresh) to avoid introducing weed seeds

Mulching

Mulches provide surface insulation to help conserve moisture, modify soil temperature, and provide weed control. Apply mulch in late June, after soil is thoroughly warmed.

Flower gardens enjoy oak leaf mulch. Their addition will aid water absorption and water holding ability.

Organic additives worked into the soil prevent compaction and greatly improve aeration. Mulches and other organic additives are not fertilizers; if they are not completely broken down when they are worked into the soil, they will tie up soil nitrogen during their breakdown. This may result in poor plant growth and the need for additional nitrogen fertilizer.

Before applying the mulch, water well; be sure that any crust on the soil surface has been broken and all weeds have been hoed out; then, it may be wise to apply a top dressing of a good garden grade fertilizer (10-10-10).

The mulch should be applied two or four inches deep, but do not pile mulch high around the plant stem.

Seeds for Thought

Spring
- Black plastic laid over freshly tilled soil will warm the soil and give plants a good start. Cut a hole for each plant, leaving space to water. In July, cover plastic with compost or grass clippings.
- Gardeners should resist the temptation to work the soil too early in spring, when the soil is often wet. Working wet soil can compact it, pushing out valuable air pockets and creating large soil clumps. Not only is aeration reduced, but the soil can become hard and cement-like. To tell if the soil is ready to be worked, take a handful and squeeze it. If the soil becomes a wet ball of mud the soil is obviously too wet and may need organic matter added to it. The soil is ready to work when the soil ball breaks up easily after squeezing it.

Summer
- Feeding both vegetables and flowers is important at this time of year. Overfeeding is just as bad as not feeding at all. If you want leaves, feed the plants a lot of nitrogen. If it's blooms you want, it might be best to skimp on nitrogen. Stems and roots need potash and phosphate for strong development. Both of these, especially the phosphate, will help flowers to form and bloom. Adequate nitrogen improves the quality of your foliage, but if your soil is heavy, keep in mind that a small amount will last a long time. Many new gardeners overfeed their annuals and have more leaves than flowers.
- If your flower garden has extremely healthy looking plants producing only a few flowers, check your fertilizer mix. Many gardeners automatically use a 10-10-10 food formula. Some should be using a 5-20-20 formula or even a 9-45-30. A soil test is definitely in order. Check with your local county Extension Service.

Fall
- Allow the surface of the turned-over garden to remain rough to achieve maximum benefit from the freeze-thaw cycle.
- Hold off applying all winter cover until the ground has received a permanent hard crust. Beginning gardeners often labor under the assumption that the main purpose of winter cover is to keep the plants warm. In reality, winter cover is used to stabilize the soil temperature, to prevent violent fluctuations in temperature. It is far better to cover late than too early.

THE NORTHERN GARDENER'S LIBRARY

Chapter 2

Perennials

Creating the Perennial
Masterpiece

Popular Perennials

Shade Gardens

Rock Gardens

Creating the Perennial Masterpiece

Glenn Ray

Of all the gardening arts, creating the exceptional perennial flower garden is among the most challenging and rewarding. Perennial, in the northern gardener's vocabulary, usually refers to those herbaceous (non-woody) plants that are capable of surviving in their outdoor location for more than two years.

The gardener's usual goal in developing the perennial flower garden is to arrange these plants to produce a picturesque effect. At first thought one might believe the task is one of simply setting perennials into the garden for display and keeping them healthy, with the desired effect automatically achieved. Such a display might be pleasing, for just about any assortment of flowers has a certain beauty, but perennials differ greatly in their habit and in what they can contribute to the garden. Some grow tall and round and become red or pink for awhile. Others stay close to the ground. Some develop a heavy appearance, others stay delicate and feathery. Some turn blue in July, some not until August. Ideally the gardener

should know well what each member of the perennial garden is capable of performing, both as an individual and in chorus.

With their majestic spires, delphiniums make an excellent background planting. (MSHS)

Although it is a picture that is desired, the creator of the exceptional perennial garden must become more a choreographer than a painter or sculptor. Perennial flowers are not fixed as a portrait on canvas or a form in stone. They are alive, and throughout the growing season are constantly changing from one day to the next. A choreographer, my dictionary tells me, "is a person who creates dance compositions and plans and arranges dance movements and patterns for stage dance." Similarly, the artistic challenge to the perennial garden "choreographer" is to create compositions from living, growing, changing objects of varying colors, forms, and sizes to produce harmony of movement, of form, and pattern on the garden stage.

Although some very beautiful perennial gardens can be created by concentrating on specific forms and textures, we usually look to the perennial garden for color. Very few of even the best perennials are in bloom for more than three weeks, so a sequence of blooms is required to maintain color throughout the season. To keep the perennial garden colorful from April to October, one should know the approximate flowering dates and blossom color of each potential member of the garden. Even then Mother Nature has a way of interfering with the expected stage entrances of flowers in bloom. Variability of weather, differences in soil, moisture, light, and temperature requirements can sometimes make our garden perennials miss their cues.

Lilies can provide vibrant mid-summer color to any garden. (MSHS)

The following list of perennials, found hardy in the Twin Cities area, was compiled to help the northern gardener decide which perennials are best for his or her garden. (Expanding on the rather loose definition that began this article, we've included some bulbs, and even trees and shrubs, to round out the flowering seasons.)

21

Early Spring

Plant	Height	Color
Snowdrop (*Galanthus spp.*)	L	W
Crocus (*Crocus spp.*)	L	Y,W,P
Hepatica (*Hepatica acutiloba*)	L	W,Lb
Chionodoxa (*Chionodoxa lucilae*)	L	B
Scilla (*Scilla sibirica*)	L	B
Winter Aconite (*Eranthis spp.*)	L	Y
Bloodroot (*Sanguinaria canadensis*)	L	W
Puschkinia (*Puschkinia scilloides*)	L	W,Lb
Greigi tulips (*Tulipa greigi*)	L	R,Y
Nanking Cherry (*Prunus tomentosa*)	Shrub	W
Dutchman's Breeches (*Dicentra cucullaria*)	L	W
Moongold apricot (*Prunus armeniaca 'Moongold'*)	Tree	W
Yellow Bells (*Uvularia grandiflora*)	M	Y
Species tulips (*Tulipa spp.*)	M	R,O,W,Y,P,Pk
Flowering Plum (*Prunus triloba*)	Shrub	Pk
Bergenia (*Bergenia cordifolia*)	M	Rose,Pk
Mertensia (*Mertensia virginiana*)	M	B
Anemone (*Anemone pulsatilla*)	L	P
Creeping Phlox (*Phlox subulata*)	L	Pk,Rose,W
Brunnera (*Brunnera macrophylla*)	M	B
Bleeding Heart (*Dicentra spectabilis*)	T	Pk
Leopard's Bane (*Doronicum cordatum*)	M	Y
Rockcress (*Arabis caucasica*)	L	W
Narcissus, Daffodils (*Narcissus spp.*)	M	Y,W
Toka Plum (*Prunus 'Toka'*)	Tree	W

Late Spring

Plant	Height	Color
Toka Plum (*Prunus 'Toka'*)	Tree	W
Trillium grandiflorum	M	W
Underwood Plum (*Prunus 'Underwood'*)	Tree	W
Nodding Trillium (*Trillium cernuum*)	M	W
Hyacinth (*Hyacinth orientalis*)	L	Y,W,B,Pk
Fritillaria (*Fritillaria imperalis*)	T	Y,P
Dwarf iris (*Iris spp.*)	L	P
Jacob's Ladder (*Polemonium reptans*)	M	B
Grape Hyacinth (*Muscari botryoides*)	L	W,Lb
Iceland Poppy (*Papaver nudicaule*)	M	Y,O
Aubrieta (*Aubrieta deltoides*)	L	Pk
Shooting Star (*Dodecatheon meadia*)	L	W,Rose-Pk
Candytuft (*Iberis sempervirens*)	L	W
French Lilac (*Syringa spp.*)	Shrub	W,Rose,P,Lav,Pk
Trollius (*Trollius europaeus*)	T	Y,O
Bearded Iris (*Iris spp.*)	M-T	W,O,B,Y,Pk,Rose,P
Gasplant (*Dictamnus albus*)	T	W,Pk
Lily of the Valley (*Convallaria majalis*)	L	W

Summary

Plant	Height	Color
Lily of the Valley (*Convallaria majalis*)	L	W
Columbine (*Aquilegia spp.*)	M	Mixed
Peony (*Paeonia spp.*)	M	R,Y,W,Pk,Rose
Centaurea (*Centaurea montana*)	M	P,B
Shasta Daisy (*Chrysanthemum leucanthemum*)	M	W
Oriental Poppy (*Papaver orientale*)	M	R,O
Acris (*Ranunculus acris*)	M	Y
Centranthus ruber	M	Rose
Maltese Cross (*Lychnis chalcedonica*)	T	Scarlet
Lysimachia (*Lysimachia punctata*)	M	Y
Evening Primrose (*Oenothera fruticosa*)	L	Y
Baptisia (*Baptisia australis*)	T	Pb
Thermopsis (*Thermopsis caroliniana*)	T	Y
Hardy Shrub Rose (*Rosa rugosa hybrid*)	Shrub	W,P,R,Y
Campanula glomerata	M	Pb
Lupine (*Lupinus polyphyllus*)	M	Mixed
Achillea 'Coronation Gold'	M	Y
Campanula persicifolia	M	W,B
Coral Bells (*Heuchera sanguinea*)	M	Rose,W,Pk
Canterbury Bells (*Campanula spp.*)	T	Pk,W,B,P
Foxglove (*Digitalis spp.*)	T	Mixed
German Catchfly (*Lychnis viscaria*)	M	Rose
Filipendula (*Filipendula rubra*)	T	W,Pk
Delphinium (*Delphinium elatum*)	T	B,P,Pk,Rose,W
Lily (*Lilium spp.*)	M,T	W,O,Y,Rose,R
Agrostemma (*Agrostemma coronaria*)	M	P,Rose
Linum (*Linum perenne*)	M	B,W
Veronica 'Crater Lake Blue'	M	B
Baby's Breath (*Gypsophila paniculata*)	M	W

Summer (cont.)

Plant	Height	Color
Coreopsis (*Coreopsis grandiflora*)	T	Y
Daylily (*Hemerocallis spp.*)	T	Y,O,M,Pk
Astilbe (*Astilbe spp.*)	M	W,Rose,Pk
Veronica 'Icicle'	M	W
Summer Phlox (*Phlox decussata*)	T	W,Rose,Pk,Lav
Monkshood (*Aconitum spp.*)	T	B,P
Achillea ptarmica 'Pearl'	M	W
Clematis (*Clematis spp.*)	Vine	W,R,P,Pk
Statice (*Statice latifolium*)	M	Pb
Bee Balm (*Monarda didyma*)	M	R,Pk
Balloon Flower (*Platycodon grandiflorum*)	M	Pb,W,Pk
Butterflyweed (*Asclepias tuberosa*)	M	O

Gardening Skill

Removing faded flowers, "deadheading", is an essential summer activity if you want to prolong the bloom of your perennial garden and maintain its appearance.

Deadheading works like this: When most flowers fade, they go to seed and that's the end of the plant's life cycle for the season. When you remove the flowers before the seeds form, the plant keeps trying to produce seed by producing new flowers. You end up prolonging the bloom even though this second showing of flowers may not be as large as the first.

Even if a plant won't keep flowering, faded blooms should be removed. Seed production requires a lot of energy, and unless you want the seeds, this energy would be better used by the plant in building up a stronger root system for next year.

Late Summer

Plant	Height	Color
Butterflyweed (*Asclepias tuberosa*)	M	O
Sedum (*Sedum spp.*)	L	Pk,Y,W
Purple Coneflower (*Echinacea purpurea*)	M	P
Blackberry lily (*Belamcanda chinensis*)	M	O
Heliopsis (*Heliopsis scabra*)	T	Y
Anthemis (*Anthemis tinctoria*)	M	Y
Echinops (*Echinops ritro*)	T	B
Centaurea macrocephala	T	Y
Liatris (*Liatris spp.*)	T	P,W,Rose
Jerusalem Artichoke (*Helianthus tuberosus*)	T	Y
Hosta (*Hosta spp.*)	L,M	W,Lav-B
Rudbeckia (*Rudbeckia spp.*)	M	Y
Hibiscus (*Hibiscus moscheutos*)	T	Pk,W
Golden Glow (*Rudbeckia laciniata 'Hortensa'*)	T	Y
Bottle Gentian (*Gentiana andrewsii*)	M	Pb,B
Physostegia (*Physostegia virginiana*)	T	Pk
Helenium (*Helenium spp.*)	M	Y
Turtlehead (*Chelone spp.*)	T	W,Rose
Solidago (*Solidago spp.*)	M,T	Y
Fall Aster (*Aster spp.*)	M,T	P,W
Chrysanthemum (*Chrysanthemum spp.*)	M	W,Y,O,Pk,Rose,M

Key: Height
T - Tall (Over 3 feet)
M - Medium (1-3 feet)
L - Low (Under 1 foot)

Key: Color
O - Orange
R - Red
P - Purple
Pk - Pink
W - White
Y - Yellow
Lav - Lavender
B - Blue
Lb - Light blue
Pb - Purplish blue
M - Maroon

Popular Perennials

Ainie Busse and Charlie King

[Over the years, *Minnesota Horticulturist* has asked gardeners to tell us about favorite perennials, either personal favorites or the ones they see most commonly grown as they travel and work throughout the state. This article was drawn from two "ten best" lists by Ainie Busse and Charlie King. Four plants made both lists, while the others received only singular acclaim. It wasn't enough for Alnie and Charlie to tell us which ones they liked best; we wanted to know why.]

Ainie: A perennial flower garden is an attractive alternative to an annual garden, since perennials do not need to be replaced each year. Planning is needed, however, to have continuous bloom in the perennial garden. In addition to period of bloom, other factors to consider are plant height, bloom color and size, foliage and site preference for full sun, full shade, or partial shade.

I've chosen a list of perennials for northern gardens that, in my experience, are the most popular with the average gardener. I have not included tulips, daffodils, and other bulbs that are not propagated for resale in northern states. Some gardeners are "collectors" and specialize in only one kind of perennial, but most backyard gardeners, I think, enjoy having a variety of perennials.

Charlie: Many times, in conversations with fellow gardeners, I have heard it said: "I am going all out with perennials this year." The connotation seems to be that they are looking for a maintenance-free garden. Nothing could be further from the truth. Whether it be perennials, annuals, or vegetables, plan on spending the necessary time to nurture and care for that garden, or the results will be disappointing.

As with any type of gardening, it is helpful to start with hardy, time-proven plants to increase your chances of success. This is my list of favorite perennials for the flower garden. It should be helpful to anyone who is planning to start a perennial border this year, expanding or enhancing an existing one, or just getting into perennials and in need of a few plants to get started.

This selection offers garden color from early spring to late summer. As you become better acquainted with perennials, you will soon realize that not any will bloom continuously throughout the season. The garden is an ephemeral setting and so relies on the mastery of the gardener to blend the many transitions of color and texture as the season progresses.

Baby's Breath

Close to the top of the list in popularity is baby's breath, *Gypsophila paniculata,* grown as much or more for its use in arrangements or drying, as for its presence in the garden. The average height is three feet and it seems to like some limestone in the soil. Baby's breath does best in full sunlight and generally blooms from June through August, depending on the cultivar. Gardeners like the feathery, mist-like look; the flowers are ideal for flower arranging. *G. paniculata florepleno* is the species most often found in garden centers. For drying, baby's breath should be cut before the blossoms begin to fade and hung upside down in a cool, dark area of a building. [AB]

Bleeding Heart

This old favorite is reminiscent of grandma's garden of years gone by. The bleeding heart, *Dicentra spectabilis*, produces dainty, heart-shaped pink and white flowers on graceful stems in May. The plant grows to a height of two feet and likes good drainage. Bleeding hearts do best in partial shade, but can be grown in full sun. The fleshy roots can be divided as soon as the foliage has turned yellow, sometime in mid-summer. This plant is a must for the mixed border. [CK,AB]

Chrysanthemums

By selecting the proper chrysanthemum hybrids, one can have bloom from June until frost. *Chrysanthemum x superbum* (sometimes called *maximum*), or shasta daisy, blooms from June until September. It prefers full sun and should be divided every two years before the roots become overcrowded. The shasta daisy usually has a yellow center, or crest, and has one or more rows of white rays ranging in size from two inches to seven inches across. Height can vary from 12 inches to three feet.

Chrysanthemum coccineum, or painted daisy, (sometimes called *Pyrethrum*) is a lovely cut flower and border plant that blooms in June and July. The painted daisy will bloom again if cut back after the first bloom and will tolerate partial shade. The average height is two feet, and colors range from

Hardy fall mums are often the focal point in the late-season garden. (MSHS)

ple, pink, red, and white to blends of these colors with white. They range in size from the 15-inch columbine suitable for the rock garden to the stately three-foot variety that is well adapted to any mixed border. It is advisable to raise new plants from seed to replace those that have deteriorated with age. Dividing or separating mature plants does not usually produce satisfactory results. [CK]

Daylily

The daylily, *Hemerocallis*, has been the focus of much hybridizing activity. The newer introductions are so vastly improved over the species seen growing along the roadways that they are hardly recognizable as the same flower. The daylily needs little care, is adaptable to most soils, tolerates heat and drought, and grows in sun or semi-shade. Daylilies are easily propagated by root division and can be transplanted just about any time from spring to fall, even in full bloom. Many cultivars begin blooming in June and others continue blooming until frost, but the peak daylily bloom in Minnesota occurs during the last two weeks in July.

Daylilies have an amazing range of colors, capturing almost every hue except pure blue and pure white. The plants range in height from 10 inches to five feet or more. There are miniatures and large-

pink to ruby-red.

A series of hardy fall mums has been bred specifically for the Upper Midwest by the University of Minnesota. These cultivars extend the period of bloom in the garden from August well into October, and can survive light frosts in the fall. For best results in overwintering, cover with a layer of mulch. [AB]

Columbine

This delightful perennial offers a bloom period of a month or more in early summer. Columbines, *Aquilegia*, grow well in full sun to partial shade. Colors range from solid shades of yellow, blue, pur-

Mass plantings of daylilies provide a profusion of color. (MSHS)

flowered types. Flower forms are variously described as flat, round, spider, cupped, recurved, ruffled, ribbed, or double. Texture can be smooth or velvety. There's not much chance of trying every cultivar, as there are over 10,000 registered hemerocallis. [AB]

Delphinium

Without any doubt, the delphinium is the queen of the perennial border from June to July. There is no other perennial more stately. If you are in search of true blue for your border, search no more, for you will have discovered wonderful blues in the varieties 'Blue Bird', 'Summer Skies', and 'Blue Jay'. When grown in clusters of three or more in a mixed border they are magnificent, and all the more so when these dazzling blues coincide with the oranges and yellows of lilies. Because of their height, delphiniums will require some means of support. They are also heavy feeders, and will require a rich, well-prepared soil, to which a copious amount of compost has been added. [CK]

Hibiscus or Garden Mallow

This is a summer-blooming perennial of unbelievable color and size. The gardener will find that this perennial will make the garden come alive when all else is fading. It is easily started from seed sown during the winter months. The popular cultivar 'Southern Belle' requires extra attention in late autumn to assure its survival through the winter. This can be easily accomplished by removing the canes and mounding soil over the crowns. Bags of leaves will provide that extra margin of protection. The garden hibiscus is at its glorious best starting about the third or fourth year after planting. [CK]

Iris

The Iris genus is sub-divided into many interesting groups. The most well known is the tall, bearded variety which blooms from late

May to early June. Once you become accustomed to growing iris, I suggest you look beyond this type to other groups, which will extend the bloom time on both ends. Flower color is found in soft pinks, good blues, yellows, whites, dark purple, and warm shades of brown, with blends of everything in between. The one color not to be found in the Iris genus is true red. Separate mass plantings seems to be the most effective way to plant iris due to the rather dowdy post-bloom appearance that lends little to a neat, mixed perennial border. If you do use them in your perennial bed, plant a later blooming plant in front of the iris to mask the foliage. Irises are propagated by rhizomes, which should be planted in a well-drained soil in late summer.

The beardless Siberian iris is gaining wide popularity, since it blooms in June and July. These iris, which resemble orchids, are ideal for arranging. Their long, graceful foliage makes an excellent backdrop for the garden and for companion plants. Siberian iris are easy to grow, do well in sun or shade, and are easily propagated by root division from late August through September. They can tolerate moist conditions and need moisture until they get established. The average height is 30 to 36 inches, but some cultivars are shorter. The color range includes white, varying

Separate mass plantings are the most effective way to display the iris. (D. Emerson)

shades of blue, violet, wine, purple, lavender, rose, and yellow, as well as bicolors and bitones. The Siberian iris make beautiful landscaping plants in mass plantings. [AB,CK]

Leopard's-Bane

This hardy, spring-blooming perennial's flowering coincides with the mid- and late-flowering tulips. The yellow daisy-like flowers on long, straight stems are suitable for use as a cut flower. This plant is easily started from seed in late winter. The best know variety is Doronicum cordatum. [CK]

Lily

The lily, *Lilium*, is the true aristocrat of the perennial border. The gardener would do well to utilize the many wonderful characteristics of this plant, especially its prolonged bloom period. A mixed border which includes lilies results in the zenith of perfection by mid-July. Lilies are easy to grow, providing they have a well-drained soil. They are sun-loving, but will tolerate light shade. Some shade is even beneficial during the bloom season to prolong the flower color. Lilies are heavy feeders and respond favorably to a spring application of 10-20-20 fertilizer. October is the best time to plant lilies.

Lupine spires punctuate the early-summer garden. (MSHS)

Lilies are being grown by more northern gardeners each year. Among the most popular are the Asiatic hybrids. They make ideal cut flowers, and vary in height from approximately 20 inches to over five feet. The taller cultivars have excellent garden value. They are easy to grow and the flowers are described as upfacing, outfacing, or downfacing. Colors are in varying hues of red, orange, yellow, pink, maroon, cream, and white. Some petals are heavily spotted and others are without spots. There are now several hundred registered hybrids. [AB,CK]

Lupine

This perennial of many-colored spires blooms for a period of four to six weeks from late spring through early summer. Lupines have been vastly improved by means of cross-breeding and selection, so the present-day gardener has the benefit of exquisite colors combined with robust plants. It is best to plant them in the back of the border because of their messy appearance once the flowers are done. This situation calls for the gardener to become a bit creative by interplanting later-blooming perennials that will conceal the untidy leaves of the lupines.

In order to grow lupines to perfection, the soil should be enriched and prepared deeply. Lupines have a substantial taproot and it is best not to transplant them once they have become established. Pruning away the spent blooms is a mistake, for it forces the development of new shoots that yield a few weak spikes in late summer. To prevent seed production, it is better to strip away the green seed pods with a downward motion of the thumb and forefinger, allowing the spent spikes to remain intact. [CK]

Monarda or Bee-Balm

If I were to say that monarda is the "vagabond" of the mixed border, you might envision a perennial that is invasive and much too troublesome to hold under control. There's some truth to this, but I like the roving characteristics of monarda in the garden. It has a very subtle long-range effect on a mixed border. As monarda moves out from its original planting site, it has the ability to blend well with other perennials. Monarda spreads and propagates by shallow, underground stolons which can be easily removed from those areas where it's unwanted. Over the years monarda has grown on nearly every square foot in our garden at one time or another. The midsummer color, especially the red shades, is outstanding and persists for about three weeks. Three improved garden varieties — 'Cambridge Scarlet', 'Croftway Pink', and 'Mrs. Perry Crimsonred'

— have been developed. All three flourish in ordinary garden soil. Spring is the preferred time to plant monarda. [CK]

Peony

This popular perennial of unusual beauty blooms from late May to mid-June. Our northern climate is well suited to the culture of peonies, *Paeonia*. In fact we are envied by gardeners in warmer climates who find they are unable to grow the peony successfully. They are extremely hardy and easily grown, provided they receive full sun, plus the added benefit of no competition from nearby shrubs or trees.

The soil should be rich and deep; in light, poor soil, the plants will become weak and flower sparsely. Peonies take several years to become established, but once they are, they can be left undisturbed for up to 30 years. It is best to use peonies in small, informal settings where they can develop to their fullest, rather than in a mixed perennial bed where they occupy a disproportionate amount of space after they've finished blooming, although the foliage remains handsome throughout the summer. September is the best time to plant peonies; however, a successful planting can be achieved in early spring with care. The depth of the planting is crucial and 'eyes' should not be more than two inches below the soil line. Planting too deep is a common cause of failure with peonies.

Peonies are classified as single, Japanese, semi-double, anemone, double, and hybrid. There is a wealth of fine cultivars, and many are moderately priced and available to the average gardener. Peonies are making a stunning comeback after a long hiatus in some gardens. [AB,CK]

Phlox

Among the favorites for summer blooming flowers are the tall phlox, *Phlox paniculata*. These generally bloom in July and August, but some will begin in June while others continue into September. Many are fragrant and most grow to about three-feet tall and do best in full sun. During hot, humid summer days, powdery mildew on the leaves can be a problem, so a spray of a fungicide every ten days is suggested for control. A miticide prevents deformed blossoms. Phlox are easily divided by root division in the spring or fall.

Colors range from pink to red and from white to purple. The blue colors benefit from partial shade as they tend to fade in the sun. To induce flowering and to prevent reseeding, the flower clusters should be cut off after blooming.

The spring-blooming creeping phlox, *Phlox subulata*, sometimes referred to as moss pinks, forms four- to six-inch mats and is a favorite for slopes, banks, borders, edges, or under shrubs, especially since it is semi-evergreen. The bloom period is April and May. [AB]

Rudbeckia makes a fine cut flower from late-summer blooms. (MSHS)

Rudbeckia

Rudbeckia is known by the names coneflower and black-eyed susan, and occasionally, gloriosa daisy. Rudbeckias prefer a sunny border, but will do well in partial shade. They are fine cut flowers and bloom from July into September. They grow easily from seed or can be planted by root division in the spring. [AB]

Shade Garden Perennials

Michael Heger

Almost anyone can grow flowers in a sunny location, but many gardeners, when confronted with a shady spot in the garden, throw up their hands in despair. They think they must either chop down their trees or give up entirely. However, there are a great many plants that actually prefer shade to sunlight.

For simplicity, shade can be divided into the following categories:

Open shade might be thought of as a shaded site that is exposed to the sky, where light intensities are relatively high, but where air and soil temperatures are considerably lower than in full sun. A good example of this is a site located just outside the drip line of a tree or on the north side of a building.

Partial shade is roughly equivalent to open shade in the amount of light received. It may be a situation where there is sun for a portion of the day, or where a plant receives dappled sunlight over the entire day, as under the crown of certain trees.

Dense shade is usually found under the low-hanging branches of such thickly foliaged trees as the Norway maple. Dense shade almost inevitably is accompanied by surface tree roots which can rob the perennials of moisture and nutrients. Maples, willows, and poplars are especially noted for this. Dense shade should be avoided because of root competition and because light intensities are usually too low for most plants to survive.

The ideal situation for shade-loving perennials is one that falls in the range of open to partial shade. In other words, these plants should receive little or no direct sunlight, but light intensity should remain relatively high.

The optimum soil for these plants is a well-drained, fertile, loam soil that is relatively free of tree roots. Existing soil conditions in the garden may limit the kinds of shade-loving perennials that can be planted; however, soil can be modified by the addition of organic matter.

Aconitum (Monkshood)

The chief value of this genus is its hardiness, dark glossy foliage, and minimal care requirements once established. Blue or purple flowers are usually produced in August and September and are good for cutting. There are very few fall-blooming perennials with blue flowers. It should be noted that all parts of these plants are poisonous if eaten. Some of the tallest varieties may need staking. They are best planted in the middle or back of the border, about two feet from other plants.

Astilbe (False Spirea)

Astilbes are among the best perennial flowers for shade. They possess many fine qualities including an extensive color range, excellent form, and attractive foliage that lasts through the entire growing season. They have become identified with waterside plantings because of their need for a fertile, moist soil. However, they will not tolerate a soil that remains saturated in winter.

The flowers appear during June and July in dense panicles on stems about two feet tall. There is a dazzling array of pastel colors available, ranging from pink to red to purple and white.

To maintain the most vigorous plants with maximum size flowers, the plants should be divided about

Nothing beats astilbes for lasting beauty in the shade garden. (MSHS)

every third year in spring. Astilbes are effectively used in groups of three in a perennial border or massed in shady locations as a ground cover.

Bergenia (Megasea)

These Asiatic perennials, although somewhat coarse in appearance, deserve a place in the garden. They are particularly valued for their 10-inch, evergreen, cabbage-like leaves. For this reason, they are often recommended as edging plants or as ground covers for small areas. The foliage persists throughout the year but takes on a reddish tint in winter. Bergenias spread by rhizomes on the surface of the ground but they do not grow excessively fast.

Spikes, resembling hyacinths, bloom in late April and May on one-foot stems that rise out of the foliage. Flower production is often poor after a severe winter. Bergenias perform best in a fertile, moist soil, planted in groups spaced one foot apart. Division every third or fourth year is recommended.

Chelone (Turtlehead)

This is a genus of several species, all of which are native to North America. They are excellent plants for a moist soil in open shade. They are easy to grow and have few insect or disease problems. Foliage is a shiny, dark green and remains attractive throughout the growing season. Flowers, whose shape resembles that of a turtle's head, appear in short terminal clusters during August and September. Being rather vigorous growers, turtleheads are most impressive when planted as single specimens in the garden. They may need division about every fourth year.

Cimicifuga (Snakeroot)

The rugged permanence of these stately plants should encourage their use as specimens in the herbaceous border. The long racemes of small white flowers are held well above the shiny compound leaves, reaching heights that vary from three to eight feet. There are no serious insect or disease problems. Division is unnecessary unless you wish additional plants.

Epimedium (Barrenwort)

With increasing interest in ground cover plants, the Epimediums have come into their own. Barrenworts are chiefly valued for their attractive varicolored foliage and the fact that they make a beautiful, slow-spreading ground cover. The small, cup-shaped flowers appear in early spring, with colors ranging from white to yellow, red or rose, depending on the variety. The leaves appear after the flowers and are semi-evergreen. It is best to cut the old foliage to the ground in early spring to show off the flowers and the new foliage.

Epimediums respond best in a shady location with a loam soil. Extremely dry places should be avoided. They are very long-lived and division should only be necessary to increase the number of plants. This can be done in early spring or early fall. There are no important pest or disease problems.

Ferns

Ferns in the garden are a delight at any time during the growing season. In spring, the delicate fiddleheads bring life to the garden long before most other plants have broken dormancy. Their lush green foliage in summer helps to accentuate the cool, inviting appearance of the shady garden. And in fall, the brown hues of the deciduous types add interest.

As a general rule, most ferns relish a slightly acid, loam soil. The soil should contain ample amounts of peat moss or leaf mold. Moisture is essential to prevent leaf scorch, but poor drainage is fatal to most ferns. The application of a mulch each spring will be a great aid to moisture conservation. Fertilizers are not essential, but most ferns will respond to very dilute solutions of organic fertilizers. Ferns can be left undisturbed in one spot for many years.

Filipendula (Meadow Sweet)

Filipendulas are grown for their attractive fern-like foliage and their feathery terminal flower clusters. Most of them are large and best used as background plants. Flowers appear in June and July and are pink or white according to variety.

A moist soil with high organic content in open or partial shade is ideal. Cutting the stems back after flowering will produce a mound of

Starting early in the season, ferns with their lush, feathery foliage add a softness and inviting charm to the shade garden. (MSHS)

fresh foliage. Plants are best seen as single specimens near the back of the garden where they can be left alone for many years.

Helleborus niger (Christmas Rose)

Despite what the common name suggests, this plant does not bloom during the Christmas season in northern states. Weather conditions govern the start of bloom, which in this area is usually early to mid-April. Helleborus will remain in bloom for at least a month. Plants are usually 12 to 15 inches tall with dark green, leathery foliage. Blooms are white, faintly flushed with pink as they age, and make an attractive cut flower.

A cool, moist, partially shaded location is best, with abundant organic matter to maintain moist conditions. Plants, though slow to establish, are long-lived and are best left undisturbed.

Hosta (Plantain Lily)

Hostas are among the finest perennials for the shady garden. They have all the qualities desired in a low-maintenance perennial: hardiness, longevity, freedom from insects and diseases, beauty, and charm. In the past, hostas have been grown mainly for their foliage, but with the introductions of improved flowering varieties, their attractive flowers are being appreciated by many gardeners.

Beautiful foliage makes hostas an excellent choice for the shade. (MSHS)

The bloom season stretches from late June into September, depending on the varieties chosen.

Hostas are rather undemanding in their cultural requirements, and prefer a moist, loam soil of average fertility in open or partial shade. Good drainage is a must, especially in winter. Flower stalks should be removed after blooming, since they may set seed and are apt to produce unwanted seedlings in the garden. Most hostas can be used very effectively as specimens, accent plants, or borders in the garden. There is no need for frequent division of most varieties.

Lobelia

Lobelias are prized for their spires of bright flowers which bloom from summer to early fall. The plants themselves are a bit transitory, but they often seed themselves in quantity. A moist, loam soil in open shade suits them well, and an annual mulch seems to aid longevity. It may be wise to grow a few seedlings each year in order to assure a continuing display.

Mertensia virginica (Virginia Bluebells)

This is one of the prettiest blue flowers for the spring garden. The stems grow about 18 inches tall and bear pink buds which open to sapphire blue flowers in early May. Bluebells like a cool, moist, shady location. They often die down by July, so place them among plants with spreading foliage. Division, best done in early fall, is only necessary for propagation.

Primula (Primrose)

This is a very large and diverse group of plants, but only a few species are highly recommended for general garden use. Almost all of them thrive in open or partial shade and require a loam soil with an annual summer mulch to maintain moist soil conditions. If grown in areas of uncertain snow cover, they should be given a winter mulch.

Beginning shade gardeners appreciate the easy-to-grow lungwort. (MSHS)

Pulmonaria (Lungwort)

These are among the easiest shade-loving plants to grow. They are highly valued for their handsome foliage and their drooping clusters of flowers which appear in late April and May. Plants grow to about nine to 12 inches.

Best results are obtained in moist, loam soils in light shade. Once established, lungworts can be left alone for many years. Division, if desired, is best done in fall. There are no pest or disease problems.

Rock Gardens

Betty Ann Mech

Do you long to grow all kinds of flowers but have garden space the size of a ping pong table? Perhaps your yard is large, but it fails to inspire you because it looks like every other yard on the block. Or do you yearn to grow wildflowers but don't know how to display them effectively? If any of these descriptions fit you, welcome to rock gardening!

Rock gardens can vary as much as those who plant them. They can be very small and filled with tiny rare plants, or they can be large, with trees and shrubs as background. But what they have in common is the use of unusual plants in a natural setting featuring rocks.

Rock garden plants. Plants considered as rock garden plants are dwarf, mostly under one foot high, and form tight carpets, buns, or rosettes of foliage that are covered with flowers in season. Because rock garden plants are usually perennial, they grow into larger specimens each year. Mountains, deserts, plains, and seacoasts, as well as streambanks, forests, and bogs are the original homes of these plants, so the gardener has a good selection of plants no matter what the conditions of the garden site. These plants often grow in harsh, rocky places in nature, so rocks provide a natural setting for them.

Rocks are not strictly necessary for growing some of these plants, but they do shelter delicate plants

Large rocks on a gentle slope protect these rock garden plantings. (MSHS)

from too much sun and keep roots cool. Their bold appearance of permanence and wildness makes rocks an attractive contrast to colorful flowers.

Most rock gardeners do not plant annuals in their gardens because they look artificial or "too civilized." Another objection is that they many grow over the young perennials which the gardener is trying to establish. The garden may look sparse the first few months, but with good care the plants will fill in their allotted spaces by the end of the season, and look better every year after that.

Site Selection. Choose a site that you can easily view and care for, in a place that receives rain and is within reach of a garden hose. Rock gardens in full to half sun can grow the widest variety of plants, but there are many unusual rock plants that prefer shade. The garden will fit in best if it forms a connection with a background, whether that background be evergreens, shrubs, fence, pond, etc. Ideally, the rock garden should be separated from the regular annual and perennial borders with their large plants.

Soil. Many of the easier rock garden plants will thrive in a wide range of soils, and you will want to start with them. Sooner or later,

Many varieties of dianthus are suitable for rock gardens. (MSHS)

however, you will want to make a home for some more unusual plants. Suitable soil is nearly the whole secret of "good luck" with rock gardening.

A well drained but moisture retentive soil with satisfy almost all plants. First dig up the site (a mechanical tiller works best) and then pick up a handful of soil and squeeze it. The ideal soil forms a fragile ball that breaks apart at the touch of your thumb. If the soil stays in a hard ball it is heavy with clay; if it falls into a shapeless mass it is sandy.

For sunny rock gardens, good soil contains approximately one part loam (garden soil containing clay), one part sand (coarse builder's sand) and one part organic matter (partially decayed compost, peat, leafmold, etc.). The texture should be coarse and open with large flecks of organic matter and fine particles that form a coating on the coarse grains when they are wet (a garden in a wet climate may need more drainage.) For a shady garden, soil should be black, moist, and humusy—about the texture of chocolate cake! To achieve this consistency, organic matter such as leafmold made from oak leaves and peat moss should compose 50 percent of the soil. The soil should hold moisture, but be well drained with no standing water. Logs can be used to guide traffic and terrace the soil in a shady garden.

You will need approximately 18 inches of developed soil to accommodate the long roots of rock garden plants. Use your own soil as a base and add what is lacking. If your is a sunny garden, for example, and you have very sandy soil, you should add six inches of clay and six inches of organic matter, If you soil is heavy clay, add six inches of sand and six inches of organic matter. Use the tiller after each layer is spread. If you have a well drained rich loam, add some sand and gravel for drainage, and also to prevent the plants from growing too tall and out of character.

To determine the amount of soil material you need to order, multiply the garden area by the depth of the material needed (determined by the proportions above). For example, if your garden is approximately 100 square feet and you need to add a six-inch or half -foot layer of sand, you multiply 100' by 1/2' for 50 cubic feet, and then divide by 27 (the number of cubic feet in a cubic yard) for approximately two cubic yards of needed sand.

Construction. After soil is prepared, it can be shaped into gentle mounds and hollows. Fill made from discarded rocks, bricks, etc, can be used to raise the level of the

Tunica saxifraga produces a cushion of pink rosettes. (MSHS)

garden, or extra soil can be prepared. Even a little height puts the plants 'on stage' where they can be more easily appreciated.

There are two basic styles of construction: formal and informal. Formal terracing and rectangular raised beds usually look best combined with man-made structures such as houses and driveways. Informal styles remind us of the wild, and may successfully be used near the home or at some distance from it. This is where you can use your creativity. For inspiration, visit rocky areas in the wild and other rock gardens and read rock gardening books.

Using rocks. Native rock harmonizes with gardens better than any exotic rocks you may be tempted to buy or collect. Limestone or sandstone, because of their porous structures, are preferred. Granite boulders are not only impervious to water, but their often rounded shape and varied colors make them difficult to work with; however, they are certainly better than no rocks at all. Above all, don't mix different kinds of rocks, as it detracts from the plants and looks unnatural.

Rocks can be bought from a stoneyard or quarry, collected from private land with permission, or recycled from landfills.

Sink rocks deeply into the soil so they are stable and look natural. Stratified limestone can be used to

Perennial geraniums give a rock garden color in late-spring. Geraniums grow best in sun or partial shade. (MSHS)

build ledges and terraces on slopes. Irregular boulders gathered into drifts resemble a dry stream bed. Choose all sizes of rocks, from large 'two-man' rocks down to fist-size. Arrange them in masses or groups that fade out to areas without rocks. Don't make a fortress of only rock, or dot them like salt and pepper all over the site.

Planting and maintenance tips. Nestle plants between rock, with spreading plants away from the cushion types. A mulch of stone ships or gravel in a sunny garden, or of chopped dry leaves in a shady garden not only discourages weeds but keeps the soil cool and moist. If you garden abuts the lawn, use a heavy permanent edging to exclude grass.

Easy rock garden plants. Local nurseries may carry a few of the more common rock garden plants, but specialty mail-order nurseries are dotted all over the country. The American Rock Garden Society operates a seed exchange for its members, Growing from seed is an easy, inexpensive way to obtain plants.

Following is a list of good plants for beginners or experts.

Alyssum
Androsace primuloides
Anemone pulsatilla
Aquilegia flabellata 'Nana'
Arabis albida
Armeria maritima
Aster alpinus
Campanula carpatica
Crocus, wild species
Dianthus, perennial types
Draba
Epimedium
Erigeron, dwarf species
Gentiana septemfida
Geranium, perennial types
Helianthemum
Hepatica
Iberis
Iris pumila and *I. cristata*
Papaver alpinum
Phlox, creeping kinds
Polemonium reptans
Potentilla aurea 'Nana'
Primula polyanthus and species
Saponaria ocymoides
Sedum
Sempervivum
Silene alpestris, S. schafta
Thymus
Tunica saxifraga
Veronica, dwarf species
Dwarf conifers and dwarf shrubs

Gardening Skill

Transplanting Tips

Transplanting seedlings into the garden always shocks young plants, but there are methods that cause plants to suffer minimal setback or growth delay. Deborah Brown of the University Agricultural Extension Service provides these suggestions:

- Start when plants are small. Annual or vegetable seedlings with four to six leaves are big enough to move.

- Transplant at sundown or on a cloudy day; wind can be as damaging as sunlight.

- Water seedlings thoroughly several hours before transplanting.

- Move seedlings with as much soil as possible around the roots.

- Plant seedlings a little lower than the surrounding soil. This forms a depression to hold water.

- Plants in degradable pots, such as peat pots or pellets, should be planted with their containers below the garden soil surface, to keep them from drying out.

- Water the soil around each transplant as soon as it is in the ground, and include a diluted starter fertilizer, made by dissolving one-half cup of 5-10-5 or 5-10-10 fertilizer in a gallon of water. Use about one-half cup of the diluted mixture for each transplant.

Gardening Skill

Propagating Perennials

Many perennials are propagated by division and separation. In herbaceous perennials the crown is the portion of the plant which produces new shoots. Lateral shoots grow each year from the base of the old stem, with roots often developing along the base of these new shoots. These new shoots flower either in the year they are produced or in the following year. As a result of this annual new growth and dieback of shoots, an extensive crown may be produced in a few years. Division of this crown is an important method of propagation and may also be necessary to prevent overcrowding of the plant.

Perennials are usually divided in the early spring or late summer. Plants which bloom in the spring and produce new growth after blooming are usually divided in the fall, while plants which produce growth in the spring and bloom in summer or fall are generally divided in the early spring.

Plants may have either a fibrous crown, such as achillea (yarrow) and chrysanthemum, or a fleshy crown, such as that of hosta (plantain lily) and campanula (bellflower). Plants with a fibrous crown usually develop a thickened, woody central crown area in two to three years. This woody portion is usually discarded, as it does not produce many shoots and eventually loses vigor.

To propagate by crown division, dig the parent plants, shake off adhering soil, and prune the shoots and roots, ensuring that each portion has at least one bud. Then separate the crown either by gently pulling apart pieces or cutting those divisions not easily pulled apart. Examples of other plants propagated by this method Include anemone (windflower), aster, dianthus (pinks), filippendula (meadowsweet), trollius (globeflower) and veronica (speedwell).

Plants such as hosta develop a fleshy compact crown which is difficult to pull apart. These plants can be propagated toward the end of their dormant period when the buds begin to grow. Dig the plants, cut apart the crown, and dust cut surfaces with a fungicide before planting. Do not allow the fleshy roots to dry out.

THE NORTHERN GARDENER'S LIBRARY

Chapter 3

Annuals

Popular Annuals

Extend the Season with Everlastings

Popular Annuals

Lawrence Rule

Perennials provide you with spots of color throughout the growing season. Flowering annuals, on the other hand, give you dazzling beds of flowers all summer. Furthermore, flowering annual displays can easily be changed each season, limited only by your imagination. Even in the short-season summers of northern Minnesota (otherwise known as Zone 3 to hardiness connoisseurs), many annuals can put on quite a show.

The flower varieties listed below are those I consider basic to a selection of flowering annuals. They are easy to grow, have dependable flowering habits, and are useful for a variety of needs. Above all else, they should, if arranged properly, do a great deal to cheer your heart and brighten up the old place. The list is a short one, and you no doubt have many others which are your personal favorites.

Sweet Alyssum (Lobularia maritima). Alyssum plants need not be purchased, for within six weeks after planting seeds, you will have blooming plants. Bloom continues until late in the fall, as light frosts do not harm this hardy little plant. When you seed alyssum, barely cover the seeds with soil, and keep moist until the plants appear. Thin the plants to about two for every running foot of border.

Alyssum does equally well in both sun and partial shade, and is tolerant of dry conditions. Expect the plant to grow as a little sprawling bush, several inches high and about a foot in diameter. Along with the basic white of the old 'Snowcloth', you can find lavender, purple, rose, and yellow colors. The plant will be covered with a myriad of tiny blooms that smell like fresh honey. If blooming wanes a little, trim the bush lightly for a fresh outpouring of blossoms.

Wax Leaf Begonia or Fibrous Begonia (Begonia semperflorenscultorum). This is a very handy flower to have around for several reasons: it grows and blooms freely in the shade, it blooms freely until killed by frost, it can be lifted in the fall to become a house plant, or you can easily

Annuals are used as fillers in bulb and perennial beds, or can be massed together to provide a dazzling display on their own. (MSHS)

take cuttings from it for indoor bloom all winter.

The east side of our house is shaded with trees, and it is there I planted a bed of 'White Tausend-schoen'. The snow-white flowers and glossy green leaves flourished all summer until killed by a cruel frost. Protected as they were near the house, they escaped the first two frosts. Little water reached them under the overhang, so we carried water to them, and each week gave them an anemic solution of 15-30-15 water-soluble fertilizer.

Wax begonias can do well in partial shade, and even in full sunshine. But why not make use of them in your shady areas? Good flowering annuals that do well in the shade are rare, while there is a whole host of sun-loving flowers. The blooms range from one to two inches in diameter, with white, pink, and red single or double flowers. Leaves may be a waxy green, variegated green, bronze, or even (ugh!) chocolate colored.

Cosmos (Cosmos bipinnatus). This annual has fallen into disfavor with some because of its rangy and untidy habits. The advent of 'Sunny Red', the 1986 All-America Selections winner, changed many opinions. 'Sunny Red' is a bush just two feet high that comes alive with bright orange-red flowers. I seeded inside under fluorescent lights on April 16, and transplanted to the flower bed on May 25. The first flower appeared on June 28, and by August the bush was covered with flowers. Visitors made 'Sunny Red' the chief conversation piece of the garden. By September 1, however, the show was over. If you haven't grown cosmos lately because of spindly growth and too few flowers, give 'Sunny Red' a try.

Geranium (Pelargonium x hortorum). The various cultivars of this variety are what come to mind when we think of geraniums. The common variety has upright growth and is two feet or less in height. It has a head of flowers, three to five inches in diameter, held up by a stiff stem. Leaves are sometimes scalloped and sometimes zoned, as with the Ringo Hybrids. Blooms are continuous, and it is no wonder they are popular, with summer colors of bright red, pink, white, and bi-colored flowers.

They tend to be bushy, and if conditions are right, will bloom until frost. Last fall we kept our geraniums blooming into November simply by moving the potted ones inside whenever the temperature dropped below freezing. Four-inch cuttings taken from the plants in September were blooming inside by December 10.

Last year I grew my geraniums from seed, starting the germinating process on March 17. The plants in three-inch pots were transplanted to their bed on May 25. 'Sprinter Hybrid White' began blooming on July 3, though 'Sprinter Hybrid Red' did not bloom until July 21. For those who believe geraniums should be seeded in December, my experience shows that a later period of seeding is not disastrous. Geranium seeds are expensive, but since almost every seed germinates, you save money by growing your own. If you purchase your plants from the nursery, inspect them carefully for disease. Take only those plants with perfect leaves.

Geranium plants can be wintered over by shaking most of the dirt off the roots and storing the plants in a root cellar. In early spring the tops can be pruned back severely and planted in the container they are to grow in during the summer. The containers are then placed outside after it warms up. I still do this with a plant or two I am fond of, but the plants sometimes tend to be woody and may develop a virus disease. Prudence would dictate purchasing plants from a reliable source, or starting with seeds.

Impatiens (Impatiens wallerana). If you have a shady place you would like to light up with a good show of blooms, think impatiens.

We have a spot on the south side of our drive that is devoid of sunshine. Furthermore it is bounded by trees. With a spade and sometimes an axe, I clean it of roots down at least six inches, and into that unlikely place impatiens are transplanted to bloom luxuriantly all summer.

Plants range from less than a foot to 1-1/2 feet high. White, red, pink, and bi-colors are offered, with a full range of pastel shades from coral to salmon to lavender. My favorite, which I grow myself, is 'Blitz', a large hybrid that bears many orange-red flowers, up to two inches in diameter. I see no real need to pinch back the modern impatiens hybrid. The new double flowers can be grown from seed and are of particular interest. Impatiens do well both as a bedding and container plant.

Lavatera (Lavatera trimestris). Not as familiar as the other flowering annuals listed, this plant has a special place where a background or screen is desired. The appearance is somewhat similar to hollyhocks, and the plants will grow to about four feet in height during our abbreviated northern Minnesota summers. The plant bears funnel-shaped flowers on its stems. If planted outside, seeds should be sown after frost in a sunny place, and thinned to stand about a foot apart in the row. For earlier bloom, start the plants inside. To date, there is not much color choice — white, pink, and rose are about the total selection. If you have trouble with hollyhocks due to a rust disease, try lavatera. They bloom by late August, and will shrug off light frosts.

Marigold (Tagetes erecta, T. patula). Last summer I had a large display of the famous 'First Lady' and the gorgeous 'Orange Lady' marigolds. These huge double flowers, large as pom-pon chrysanthemums, all but covered the leaves. I have also enjoyed the quick-blooming Janie Series and the triploid hybrid 'Red Seven Star'. Of course, if you have not yet tried 'Queen Sophia' in your garden, shame on you!

The fact is, most marigolds can be seeded directly where you want them to grow. The earliest varieties will be blooming six weeks after they are sown. You may wish to start some of the later varieties inside for earlier bloom.

The plants may be a few inches or two feet tall, the flowers little or huge, single or double, and range in color from white to deepest mahogany and everything in between. Each flower may be of a single color or may have a variety of rich colors. What is more, marigolds are easy to grow. They tolerate poor soil and drought and will bloom if left alone. Astute watering, however, as well as fertilizing, picking of spent heads, weeding, and if necessary, applying insecticides will all help the cause.

Your marigolds should take you through the heat of summer and last until the first frosts of fall.

Petunias (Petunia x hybrida). Grown as annuals in the north, like many other "flowering annuals," petunias are really perennials. Dig up a couple of your choicest plants and prune the stems back to about two inches from the roots. In a sunny window they will bloom all winter.

Petunias will flourish if pinched back during the growing season. (MSHS)

In the spring your local nursery or greenhouse will probably have a good selection of hybrid petunias in all colors of the rainbow, starting to bloom in their packs. When you plant them, it may kill you to pinch them back, losing the first blooms, but pinching the plant back a couple of times will assure you of a bushy plant and luxuriant flowering. Petunias love sunshine, but will tolerate some shade.

Grandiflora petunias have large flowers, some double, but a wet summer and driving rains will literally wash your flowers out a good share of the time, unless they are planted in a protected place. A protected planter or hanging basket may be a good way to grow your fancy grandifloras.

Multiflora petunias have smaller blooms, but many more of them. Last summer we had a small bed of multiflora petunias, 'Mixed Joy', near our front door. They gave a display of many blossoms in six different colors. There were enough flowers to satisfy the chipmunks until they grew tired of them and turned to the bird feeders. Enough water and fertilizer will keep these easy-to-grow flowers blooming all summer.

Strawflower (Helichrysum bracteatum). With the strawflower, you can have your cake and eat it, too. Strawflowers present the garden with showy blooms (actually bracts) from July to frost. Cut the flowers in their prime, tie them in little bundles, and hang them upside down in the garage until the leaves are dry. After the dried leaves are crumbled away, the flowers are ready to arrange with other dried material such as baby's breath, *Gypsophila*.

I like the mixed colors of 'Bright Bikini' (the strawflower cultivar, not the swimsuit.) I cut 'Bright Bikini' twice during the summer, though the second cutting had shorter flower stems. Strawflowers do best with sunshine and warmth. They can be direct seeded into the garden, though earlier blooms will come by using transplants.

Zinnias make an absolutely wonderful cut flower for a late summer bouquet. (MSHS)

Zinnia (Zinnia elegans, Z. Haageana, Z. linearis). Many experienced gardeners view zinnias with contempt. It seems that anyone who can grow a zucchini can grow zinnias. Along with marigolds and petunias, they are omnipresent. The bright, well-starched flowers stand taut in the hot sunshine. "Might as well grow dandelions," the gardeners sniff.

Yes, zinnias are easy to grow. They can easily be seeded where they are to stand, and they can take their share of dry weather and poor soil. Small-flowered cultivars provide early bloom. Although powdery mildew is common, breeders are working to develop a mildew-resistant strain, and it seldom interferes with the flowering of the plant.

The zinnia is an invitation for every marginal gardener — and what a selection! About every color save blue is available. You can choose tiny cultivars five inches short, or big ones 40 inches tall. You can have one-inch or six-inch diameter flowers, single or double or pom-pon, fancy and frilled.

My favorite zinnia is 'Small World Cherry', a rather small, bushy hybrid that blooms early and late with an abundance of enduring bright red flowers; 'Small World Pink' is also available.

Extend the Season with Everlastings

Esther Filson

Every fall, as I dash around my yard covering my blooming plants with blankets and sheets and whatever else I can find to protect them from a killing frost, I wonder why I didn't plant more everlastings. These plants — so named because they can be dried or preserved easily — are a much easier way to extend the season of flowering plants, and are around long after the whiteness of winter has set in.

In addition to flowering annuals and other garden plants, there are many "weedy" native plants to collect, such as goldenrod and dock found along roadsides, bittersweet and black-eyed Susans in meadows, and grasses in fields. Of course, always use common sense when collecting native plants. Do not harvest endangered plants and leave the roots of those you do collect. If your arrangement begs for a few exotic dried stems — such as magnolia and eucalyptus leaves, lotus seed pods, or Hawaiian wood roses — you're allowed a modest addition from your local florist.

Collecting

Deciding which flowers lend themselves to preserving can be perplexing. I have found experimenting with different materials to be a lot of fun, however; don't be afraid to try new things.

Flowers that aren't well suited to drying are those with petals that fall in a heap, as compared to those that shrivel and retain some of their form and color. Flowers with high water content, such as gladiolus, aren't a good bet either. Stiff-petaled flowers or colorful bracts are worth drying, as well as plants with silvery foliage. Flowers with tight center clumps dry better than loose, open-petaled types. Observing how plants bloom, die, and produce seed will help you get a sense of which flowers to pick for drying and which plants have usable pods and seed heads.

Timing is important when cutting flowers for drying. The secret is to pick them when they are just reaching maturity. The material should be as dry as possible when cut. It is best to pick on a dry day in late afternoon, after the heat of the day has passed, but before the evening dampness has set in. Select materials free from blemish-

Celosia will add color to any arrangement. (MSHS)

es and check for insect and disease damage. Strip the leaves from the stem immediately after cutting the stalk. When you have enough stems (about 10 to 12), tie them together with a rubber band or a very tightly tied string. Collect twice as much as you need to allow for breakage.

One of the tough choices when raising flowers and grasses for drying is picking them just as they are reaching their prime in the garden. To solve the problem of bare spots in the flower garden, I recommend planting twice as many plants and picking only half for drying, or placing large blooming pots in the areas lacking color.

Drying Methods

Air-drying is the easiest way to preserve plant material, although there are limits in the kinds of materials that preserve well. The essential conditions for air-drying are warmth, dryness, darkness, and good ventilation. These will speed the drying process and produce the best color in the flowers. An attic or a large closet makes a good spot. Most flowers take three to four weeks to completely air dry. In most cases, bunches of flowers dry best when hung upside down; avoid having the heads pressed upon one another.

Some flowers need to be dried in ways that will retain their natural shape. Queen-Anne's-lace and edelweiss should be dried face up on a screen with the stems hanging below. (A handy alternative is a cane chair.) Chinese lantern is easy to dry and retains its color well, but should be hooked over a string so the "lanterns" hang the way they grow. To maintain the natural curves of vines such as clematis, stretch them horizontally on a string. Grasses can be spread flat to dry or stood upright in tall containers. Make sure to pick grasses before the seed heads start to shatter. Alliums and hydrangea dry with a more open look when dried upright with their stems in a small amount of water.

Some flowers, such as strawflowers and globe amaranth, become very brittle when dried and their stems cannot support the flower heads. These need to be wired when they are picked fresh from the garden. A six to eight inch piece of 22-gauge florist wire can be inserted into the bottom of the flower head providing a false but secure stem. The stem and tissues of the flowers shrink as they dry, fastening tightly around the wire.

The use of sand, borax, silica gel, or glycerine broadens the range of flowers and leaves that can be dried, but involves a more complex process. Pressing is another method for drying foliage and some flowers. Most annuals suitable for drying can be air-dried. It's what I do with most of my plants, and what I recommend for anyone starting out.

Using Dried Plants

The real fun begins when you get ready to use the glorious array of dried plant materials indoors. Store your dried flowers in large, covered containers in a dry, dark room until you're ready to use in arrangements; this will insure their longevity.

A flower arrangement made with dried plants can fit any decor. The country look is incomplete without baskets or crocks filled with dried baby's breath, statice, or

Salvia spires add another dimension to dried arrangements. (MSHS)

a mixture of dried flowers. Indoor wreaths add charm to any decor in any season and are always popular. An attractive autumn decoration can be created from a grapevine wreath covered with accents of dried grasses, pods, yarrow, gold or orange strawflowers, bittersweet, and moss. For the Christmas season, combine flower pods, baby's breath, dried roses, glycerine-treated princess pine, and dried berries. A natural creation made from herbs such a artimesia, lavender, yarrow, salvia, tansy, and allium is perfect for a kitchen wall. A wreath covered with sea lavender, pink and blue delphiniums, roses, pastel

Wreaths are always popular and can be designed to fit any decor. (MSHS)

strawflowers, blue and pink annual statice, and globe amaranth makes a decorating statement in mauves and blues.

Wreaths can be formed around a wire frame covered with sphagnum moss secured with twine, a grapevine or straw wreath, or a Styrofoam ring covered with moss. The easiest way to secure the dried flowers onto the wreath is with a hot-glue gun.

Almost any container used for fresh arrangements can be used for dried arrangements, with the exception of clear glass (the dried stems, wires, and mechanics of assembly are best kept hidden). Baskets and terra-cotta containers are excellent; decorative ceramic containers take more care to make sure the colors coordinate and the design blends with the arrangement. Lightweight baskets may need to be anchored with sand or rocks to keep the arrangement from tipping over. To secure the flowers in the container, use florists foam; chicken wire can also be used for a less formal look.

As with fresh arrangements, follow principles of good design. Make sure there is balance, contrast, dominance, rhythm, proportion, and scale. Contrast is often difficult since the texture of the plant material is similar. Try adding smooth-surfaced pods or using glycerine-treated leaves along with the dried materials.

Other uses of dried materials include swags, flower ropes, posy-type bouquets, cornucopias, potpourris, and framed pictures. The list goes on and on — you might almost say it's everlasting.

Here is a brief listing of plants suitable for drying:

Acrolinium, sometimes known as Helipterum, is a handsome plant with flower colors in shades of apricot, pink, rose, and white. It dries best when picked before becoming fully mature and should be wired before air-drying.

Celosia, or cockscomb, comes in both crested and plumed types and both can be air-dried. They retain their color well and make a colorful contribution to any arrangement.

Gomphrena, or Globe Amaranth, is a ball-shaped flower in shades of red, white, rose, and purple. It is easily air-dried and keeps its color.

Gramineae describes the many annual grasses that are both ornamental in the garden and wonderful for drying. **Agrostis nebulosa** (cloud grass) has a wispy, delicate flower head. **Avena sterilis** is great for large arrangements. Two favorites of mine are **Briza maxima** (quaking grass), with its graceful, pendant, nodding flowers, and **Coix lacryma-jobi** (Job's tears), also used for making beads.

Helichrysum, or strawflowers, are probably the best known of all the everlastings. The flowers are very attractive, but the rest of the plant is best masked in the garden by other plantings. Remove the flowers from the stems and wire them before air-drying.

Larkspur is a lovely cut flower, either fresh or dried. 'Blue Cloud' holds its bright blue color especially well.

Limonium, or statice, is another popular everlasting. Remove the foliage before hanging to air-dry.

Molucella, or Bells of Ireland, have vivid green bracts that turn a creamy white when dried.

Nigella, or Love-in-a-mist, is easy-to-grow and has attractive white, rose, or blue flowers, followed by showy fruit capsules. The capsules and frilly foliage dry easily, and are best picked when capsules have started to open at the top. Scatter the seeds freely for next year's blooms.

Papaver, or annual poppies, have short-lived flowers that leave behind a delightful assortment of pods. Harvest and dry the pods when mature, removing the leaves from the stems.

Salvia has over 50 species and almost all can be dried. **Salvia splendens** produces a fiery red flower, **S. Farinacea** 'Victoria' is a rich medium blue, and **S. x. superba** is a deep purple.

THE NORTHERN GARDENER'S LIBRARY

Chapter 4

Bulbs

Spring Bulbs

Summer Flowering Bulbs

Spring Bulbs

Charlie King

Success with next year's spring bulbs begins in the fall. Whether your bulbs arrive by mail order or you pick them out at your local garden center, you should have them on hand no later than the first week of October. Once they arrive, it is wise to plant them as soon as possible. There's something wonderful about being able to plant something new, while the rest of the garden is showing end-of-the-season signs of age.

Bulbs have always seemed to me to contain a little bit of magic — planting something in soon-to-be-frozen ground, with no results expected for many months. If you rely on magic alone, the results may be less than expected. A bit of extra effort when the bulbs go in will bring rewards in the spring.

Planting. There are three methods for planting spring bulbs. The one I prefer involves thoroughly preparing the soil, excavating the site to a depth of 12 inches. This works best for planting large numbers of bulbs in areas where there is little existing planting. I heap the soil onto an old carpet

remnant reserved for just such occasions. The excavated soil is then blended with a generous amount of compost. Four inches of the prepared soil is returned to the planting site.

Now, let's say that I intend to plant 50 tulip bulbs of one color in this location, and that I would like to enjoy them for as many years as possible. It is imperative, then, that I place, under the bulbs, plant nutrients high in phosphorus and potash. A good ratio is 0-20-20. Note that no nitrogen is used at planting time. The recommended quantity of fertilizer is one pound for every 50 bulbs. Thoroughly blend the fertilizer into the four inches of prepared soil that has been returned to the site.

Now we're ready to set the bulbs in place. Space the bulbs five inches apart in all directions. The bottom (rooting end) of the bulbs will be eight inches below the surface when all the soil has been returned. Gently distribute the remaining prepared soil over the set bulbs. When the planting hole is half filled, water thoroughly and allow to drain. Add remaining soil

For many of us, the brilliant bloom of tulips symbolizes the month of May. Plant in large groupings for a good show of color. (MSHS)

to level off. Leftover soil can be stored for future use or used in other parts of the garden. The new planting must be kept moist up to the first hard freeze. For the first winter, it is wise to give the planting a winter cover. In subsequent winters this won't be necessary.

A second method of planting works well for planting around existing plant materials and for naturalized plantings of spring bulbs. Naturalizing can produce dramatic results, but depending on types of bulbs and conditions, replanting with new bulbs might be required at intervals. Insufficient plant nutrients and competition from turf and other plant material makes such plantings more short-lived.

Ideal places to naturalize bulbs are wooded areas, meadow strips, and places where there is no lawn or landscaping of any kind. The process can be as simple as the tossing of 10 to 20 bulbs of one variety onto a selected area and planting them where they land. With the use of a bulb planter, remove a plug of soil to the proper depth, place a bulb in, and cover with the soil from the succeeding hole, and so on. Daffodils, crocus, snowdrops, muscari, and Siberian squill all lend themselves nicely to this method.

A third method is the "procrastinating gardener's" method. This is used when a gardener has delayed

Daffodils lend themselves to irregular, naturalized plantings. (MSHS)

planting for one reason or another. Finally, at some point in mid-November or about the time of a hard freeze, a frantic effort is made to plant the neglected bulbs. This could necessitate planting them in rain or sleet or snow. No time for soil preparation; just get them into the ground the fastest way possible. The bulb planter comes to the rescue, and if the ground isn't frozen, the job can be done in a matter of minutes, and then back to the football game.

In growing spring bulbs, as in other types of gardening, doing the job right from the beginning will make the whole experience easier, more productive, and more enjoyable.

When to plant. Daffodils, hyacinths, narcissus, crocuses are the first to be planted, some time between mid-September and mid-October. These bulbs are planted two to five inches deep, according to their size, and all of them must be watered well throughout the fall. They should absorb eight to ten times their weight in water to make fall rooting and spring blooming possible.

Tulips are best planted later, from mid-October to mid-November. If the fall is long enough they can even be planted in December in unfrozen ground. All bulbs, whether spring flowering bulbs or summer flowering bulbs such as lilies, must be planted in very light, well-drained soil, and tulips should and can be planted from eight to 10 inches deep if the soil is light enough

Looking ahead to spring. After the bulbs are through blooming in the spring (trust me, they will bloom) and the flower petals have fallen, you will notice that a seed pod has formed. Remove these pods to prevent an additional drain on the already low reserve of that bulb. Make every effort to regenerate that bulb for next season.

At this point, the tops don't look very neat, but that is the case with many flowering plants after they are through blooming. Allow the foliage to remain until it turns brown and yellow, a period of about four to five weeks. During this time the foliage and bulbs should receive ample moisture and nutrients. The fertilizer must be available immediately for good results. A water soluble 20-20-20 would be most beneficial; use at the rate of one tablespoon per gallon of water.

Spring bulbs in our garden are at home in the shrub border. None are planted where annuals or perennials are grown. The old saying, "spring bulbs prefer cold winters and dry summers" is very true from our experience. Annuals and perennials do require generous amounts of moisture throughout the summer. If you desire greater

The delicate bloom of squill enhances the woodland garden. (MSHS)

mileage from your spring bulbs, perhaps you, too, should heed that old adage and not plant annuals over dormant spring bulbs.

Seeds for Thought

A dozen points to remember concerning spring bulbs:

1. Prepare the soil thoroughly.
2. Plant deep on light soil.
3. Plant shallow on heavy soil.
4. Spring bulbs require good drainage.
5. Plant quality bulbs; buy bulbs that are graded "top size".
6. All spring bulbs do best in a cool environment.
7. Most spring bulbs bloom before trees and shrubs are fully leafed out.
8. Spring bulbs love cold winters and dry summers.
9. Never plant spring bulbs against a house foundation or any hot reflective surface.
10. Plant in groups of one solid color for best effect — 10, 20, 50, or 100.
11. Plant so as to extend the season; that is, plant early, mid-season, and late varieties.
12. Practice good post-bloom culture; water and fertilize.

Planting Chart

Flower	Planting depths	spacing	Flower height
(Early season flowering)			
Chionodoxa (glory of snow)	5"	3"	VL
Crocus	5"	3"	VL
Galanthus (snowdrops)	5"	3"	VL
Hyacinth	8"	6"	L
Muscari (Grape hyacinth)	5"	3"	VL
Puschkinia (striped squill)	5"	3"	VL
Early Tulips	8"	6"	L
(Mid-season flowering)			
Daffodil	8"	6"	MH
Fritillaria imperialis	8"	12"	VH
Mid-season Tulips	8"	6"	MH
(Late season flowering)			
Allium giganteum	8"	8"	VH
Scilla sibirica (Siberian squill)	5"	3"	L
Late Tulips	8"	6"	MH/H/VH

FLOWER HEIGHT:

VL	= very low (up to 6")
L	= low (6"-12")
MH	= medium high (12"-20")
H	= high (20"-28")
VH	= very high (over 28")

The planting depth and spacing depends on the individual bulb. For specific requirements on the more common bulbs, refer to the planting chart. Generally, they are planted two and a half times deeper than their diameter. This will vary with the type of soil. With light, sandy soils, plant 1 or 2 inches deeper and on heavier clay soils, set the bulbs an inch or two more shallow. With the pointed end facing up, firmly press the bulb into the prepared soil so that the base is resting at the appropriate depth.

Summer-Flowering Bulbs

Charlie King

Through August and September, all summer-flowering bulbs, tubers, corms, and rhizomes should be at their lovely best, just in time to fill in for the fading annuals and perennials. There's a growing number of so-called summer-flowering bulbs available to gardeners through various garden centers and catalogs. Only a few are sufficiently hardy to survive our winters; the remainder are tender and must be dug in the fall and stored in a frost-proof area. If you don't want to store the bulbs, some of the more moderately priced can be treated as annuals and replaced each year.

If the bulbs blooming in your garden start with the crocus and end with late-flowering tulips, you're in for a treat. Even if you prize your gladioli, it's time to add more variety to your summer bulb collection. Begonias, dahlias, and gladioli are the traditional three, but there are more to consider.

Begonias, the tuberous types as distinct from seed begonias, are unsurpassed as a source of color and beauty in the shade garden. Their flowers, ranging from two to ten inches in diameter, come in many forms and colors. Tubers can be started indoors in March and will reach their peak bloom in July and August. The tubers are not winter hardy and must be taken indoors for the winter.

Cannas (Indian shot) is native

Large rose-like blooms of begonias create a showy display in the garden. (MSHS)

Tropical-like foliage and flower of the cannas makes a dramatic statement. (MSHS)

ing popularity. There are thousands of known varieties, from tiny pompons to giants, whose flowers can measure up to a foot and a half across. The tubers, available from local growers and catalogs, can be planted in the garden in mid-May, and will grow five to eight feet or more.

Gladiolus, commonly called "glad" for more than one reason, is a joy in the summer garden. It is easily grown and succeeds in most soils. It can be planted from early spring until July and can be found in bloom from the middle of July until frost. Requiring full sun and good drainage, today's cultivars vary greatly from the original species found in Africa, western Asia, and southern Europe.

Hardy Amaryllis (Lycoris), a beautiful bulbous plant from South Africa, is a true amaryllis with the characteristic wide strap foliage of all members of that family. The deep green foliage emerges in early spring and soon dies down and disappears. In late August the bloom spike emerges and produces a cluster of fragrant rose-pink flowers at a height of about 24 inches. This plant is sometimes erroneously referred to as the naked lily, the surprise lily, or the resurrection lily. A lily it is not! We have two large plantings of this bulb that are now 15 years old and have never failed

to South America and the West Indies. It produces strong stems from a fleshy rhizome and has large ornamental foliage (green and bronze colored) with huge showy gladiolus-like flowers. Blooming from late July to frost, cannas are sun lovers — the more sun the better. Cannas are often used in large beds of one solid color or planted in single-color groups of three to five plants each. Most varieties attain a height of three to four feet. They make a beautiful background.

Dahlias, originally from Mexico and further south, are another tender bulb of outstand-

Trumpet-shaped flowers of the amaryllis provide late summer color. (MSHS)

bulb so that the top is at a depth of about three times the diameter of the bulb. Once planted, they start a vigorous growth, foliage first followed by the bloom stalk. The flower is similar to our Easter lily, especially in its fragrance. When the bloom has finished, about mid-June, remove seed pods and keep well watered and fertilized through the remainder of the summer.

Allow the frost to kill back the foliage. If growing in the open garden, the plants must be dug without damaging the bulbs. For pot culture, store pot and all in a frost-free place, at temperatures of at least 60°F. Temperatures below this may result in no bloom next season.

to bloom. I find this bulb extremely hardy, but I give it the same generous winter cover as garden lilies.

Ismene Festalis (Peruvian daffodils), also referred to as *Hymenocallis calathina*, are native to the southern hemisphere and are also members of the Amaryllis family. They have lance-shaped foliage averaging 24 inches long and bear flowers on strong stems well above the leaves. A mature bulb is approximately the size of a large orange and will produce one bloom stalk with as many as eight to ten blooms.

Plant when all danger of frost is over, usually by late May. Plant the

Zantedeschia (calla lilies), tender rhizomes from South Africa, have arrow-shaped leaves and mainly white, pink, or yellow flowers. They can be grown in the garden or greenhouse; their main requirements are rich loamy soil and lots of moisture. Plant three inches deep and 12 inches apart in either full sun or partial shade. They are about 20 inches tall and make excellent cut flowers. Bloom time is July and August.

Advanced gardeners may want to try growing anemones, ranunculus, ixia, and sparaxis. These summer-flowering bulbs grow here, but require special care.

THE NORTHERN GARDENER'S LIBRARY

Chapter 5

Roses

All About Roses

Common Questions
About Roses

Low-Maintenance Roses

All About Growing Roses

Dorothy Campbell

You'll get no argument from me if you think the rose is the most popular of all garden flowers. (Of course, as a rose-grower of many years, I might be a bit prejudiced.) Roses give more beauty to the garden over a longer blooming time than any other flowering plant; no other flower has as long a season of bloom. The ever-changing quality of the bloom lends fascination and attraction to the rose. Every stage provides an unexpected transition, each a beauty in itself. From the exquisite bud, to the semi-open flower, to the glorious full-blown bloom, each one is rewarding.

The belief that roses require too much time and attention is just not true. They do have definite requirements, but they need much less attention than a perennial or annual bed. Their needs are not that time-consuming. In addition, improved hardiness, disease resistance, and exciting new colors have made roses more popular than ever.

The most difficult problem, if you are a novice rose grower or one with limited space for a rose bed, is which varieties to select. The rose catalogs are of no help with their gorgeous photographs and tempting descriptions. I remind myself that those catalog photos are taken of very specially selected blooms with nothing to mar their beauty; how they appear under actual garden conditions can be a completely different story.

Every year many new roses are introduced with great fanfare. The new ones seem to possess greater beauty than any previous ones. It is difficult to resist them. However, unless you have unlimited space and gardening energy, hesitate before rushing out to buy. Observe how they perform for one or two growing seasons at the various public rose gardens or in the gardens of some of the rose aficionados we have in our state. Meanwhile, it would be best to stick to the "tried and true" plants — roses that have been grown successfully in our area for at least five to ten years.

The criteria for selecting roses should be: easy care, complete dependability, profuse and recurrent bloom, disease-resistant foliage, resistance to adverse weather, and all-around good garden performance. Some of them also happen to have perfect exhibition form, but that is a bonus, not a necessary criterion. For most of us, color in the garden is more important than blue ribbons.

Some "Tried and True" Roses

Here are some excellent selections for northern gardeners, recommended by outstanding local rose growers. These roses have been grown in our area with great success, some of them for many years. The selection includes elegant hybrid tea roses and grandifloras, as well as more informal floribundas and miniatures, in a range of colors guaranteed to satisfy any palette.

Hybrid Teas: First Prize, Mister Lincoln, Pascali, Command Performance, Peace, Granada, Miss All-American Beauty, Electron, Confidence, Garden Party, Duet, Tiffany, Chicago Peace, Tropicana, Oregold, Paradise, New Day, Pristine, Patrician, Royal Highness, and Double Delight.

Grandifloras: Queen Elizabeth, Camelot, Aquarius, Pink Parfait, Sonia, Comanche, and Montezuma.

Floribundas are distinguished by flowers which are borne in large clusters. (MSHS)

Floribundas: Iceberg, Europeana, Ginger, Little Darling, Evening Star, Rose Parade, Faberge, Bahia, Fashion, Vogue, Sunsprite, Cherish, First Edition, Angel Face, Betty Prior, Apricot Nectar, Charisma, and Matador.

Miniatures: Starina, Beauty Secret, Chipper, Cinderella, Judy Fischer, Magic Carrousel, Red Imp, Rosmarin, Mary Marshall, Yellow Doll, Jet Trail, Chattem Centennial, Sheri Anne, Rise n'Shine, Pacesetter, Party Girl, Red Flush, Little Linda, Cupcake, Dreamglo, Honest Abe, Holy Toledo, Baby Katie, and Starglo.

There are many other good varieties, but these are probably the best known and most widely grown. All of these recommended roses have consistently met the criteria for good, all-around garden performance. Anyone who is just starting to grow roses or planning to add additional plants to an existing garden could not go wrong with any one of them; almost all are available at local nurseries.

April Care

April is the beginning of the year in the rose garden, whether you're uncovering last year's plants or starting to think about new ones for this year. The weather in April can be very changeable, so don't be in a mad rush to get outside to start spring chores. Wait until the weather is reasonably decent and the long-range weather forecasts optimistic. If the snow is gone from the rose beds, you can start uncovering during the first week of April, removing the leaf or hay cover. Do this in easy stages, as the ice in the covering melts.

Around mid-April, if the Minnesota Tip method of winter protection has been used, the rose bushes may be raised to an upright position. Be gentle in removing the soil from the canes, and never force the canes up if the soil is partially frozen. Wait until the soil is completely thawed. Once the plants are standing upright, firm the soil well around the base of the plants. Check the bud union (or bud graft) of the plants to make sure it is no deeper than one inch below ground level. Wash the canes off, to remove any soil remaining and any dead leaves; water plants thoroughly.

If soil mounds have been used, wait until at least the middle of April or even into the third week to remove the mounds. Be sure all danger of severe frosts has passed. Wash the soil mounds down with a gentle stream of water. Too forceful a stream can knock off developing bud growth on the canes.

Spraying or Dusting

As soon as you have uncovered your plants and washed them, spray them thoroughly with a fungicide and an insecticide, following the manufacturers' directions. Thoroughly drench the canes and soil around the plants. This is important, for disease spores and insect eggs can winter over on the canes and soil.

Spraying the plants is more effective than dusting at this time of year. If you must dust, use an all-purpose dust that contains both a fungicide and an insecticide. The label will tell you what the product contains.

After this first protective spraying or dusting, you can wait until the plants are leafed out (usually about mid-May) before starting on a regular spraying or dusting schedule. Roses should be sprayed or dusted every seven to ten days throughout the growing season.

Watering

Watch out for windy spring days that will dehydrate the newly uncovered rose canes. Get out the overhead sprinkler, and keep the rose plants well watered. Run the sprinkler for at least two hours, at least twice a week. The water will cleanse the plants of any mold, keep the canes moist, and prevent them from becoming dehydrated by the warm spring sun or strong winds. Dehydrated canes have very little chance of survival.

Planting

In our area the best time for planting roses is in the spring. Bare root plants can be planted up to May 15 or even a little bit later if the weather is cool. Potted plants should be planted after that, but not until the weather has moderated. Potted plants have usually been grown in a greenhouse and are in full leaf; they must be acclimated to outside temperature before being set in the ground.

Plant dormant (bare root) roses as soon as the soil has dried to the proper consistency to be worked. Rose plants will do well and get a good start in cold soil. Before planting a dormant rose, soak the whole plant in water for 24 hours. Always keep the roots of a new bush in water or wrapped in paper or burlap until you are ready to set it in the planting hole. Never expose the roots to wind or sun, which dries them out quickly.

Now for the planting. Dig a hole 15 to 18 inches deep and about 18 inches in diameter, depending upon the length of the shank (the part of the plant just below the bud union down to the crown of the roots) and the extent of the roots. Trim any broken or damaged roots or overly long ones.

Make a soil cone or mound in the center of the planting hole, high enough to support the shank and put the bud union about ground level or slightly below. The plant will settle down, and the union or graft shouldn't end up more than one inch below ground level. Spread the roots out and down this soil cone. The roots should go out more horizontally than vertically.

Then backfill soil around the rose roots by hand until the hole is half full. Fill the hole with water, let drain, adding more soil and more water until hole is filled. Never tramp the soil with your feet. This could damage the rose roots and compact the soil. The water will settle the soil down, filling all voids and eliminating air pockets. Firm the soil well with your hands.

Next, add loose soil, mulch, or insulating materials to cover the bud union and canes. This prevents the canes from drying out while the root system is becoming established. Large plastic pots or bushel baskets may also be used to cover the newly planted bush. Remove the cover in about 10 days, or after growth has started. Take mulch or insulating material off gently by hand, or if soil was used, wash it down with a gentle stream from the hose to avoid breaking off tender, new shoots.

Potted plants won't require this covering. The most important thing to remember when planting potted rose bushes is not to disturb the soil ball. If you do, shade with a protective covering and give it extra water.

Fertilizing

To grow good rose plants, it is very important to add some type of organic matter to your soil every spring. Organic matter is constantly being used up, so it must be added every year to all types of soil. It will improve the soil, add necessary bacteria, and encourage vigorous, lush growth.

In the latter part of April, when the ground temperature has warmed and the roots are once again able to absorb water and nutrients, work moderate amounts of organic matter into the rose bed; cultivate it into the top few inches of soil. You can use dehydrated manure, compost, milorganite, soy bean meal, alfalfa meal or pellets, etc. There are a number of local rosarians who have been using alfalfa meal or pellets on their rose beds and have been very pleased with the results. The alfalfa encourages better growth, greener leaves, and overall better blooms. It should be used in combination with a regular feeding program.

About May 1, feed established rose plants with a well-balanced, inorganic plant food, containing nitrogen, phosphorus, and potash. Follow label directions as to the amount for each plant. If you use a granular fertilizer, sprinkle it in a circle around each plant (keeping it away from the canes), cultivate it in lightly and water it in well. A liquid fertilizer may be used instead of the granular. Follow the instructions on the label of the container. Never use more than the amount recommended.

Newly planted bare root roses should not be given inorganic fertilizer until after their first bloom, around the end of June, and again in early August. Potted bushes can be treated like established plants, feeding the first of each month from May until August.

Pruning

Spring is the time for major pruning. It can be started by the latter part of April, if the weather has moderated and there seems to be no danger of severe frost. Pruning must be done when the growth buds are just beginning to swell on the canes. Pruning too early will result in the new growth being stunted by cold nights or killed by a freeze; pruning too late will result in severe shock to the plant, heavy bleeding of sap, and weakening of the plant's growth.

Before starting to prune, be sure your pruning tools are sharp. Dull pruners can do considerable damage to rose canes. The hook type of pruners and loppers is recommended rather than the anvil type, which has a tendency to crush stems. A keyhole saw is valuable to get into tight places where pruners or loppers might damage neighboring canes. Heavy leather gloves are a necessity.

How high or how low to prune depends on your personal desires and on the amount of live wood left after winter. Moderate pruning is usually recommended; this means cutting back one-third to one-half the height of the plant, depending upon the type of rose and the variety. After the pruning is done, seal the cut ends with a cane sealer, such as pure orange shellac, Tree-cote™, white glue, or even nail polish.

As summer starts, most of the work in the rose garden is behind you. Regular spraying and feeding, supplemental watering, and occasional dead-heading will be your only chores, besides picking bouquets and accepting compliments on your garden. Just don't forget to "stop and smell the roses."

Winter Care

Most roses require some winter protection if they are to survive and bloom the next year. The 'Minnesota Tip,' outlined on the next page, is one popular technique used successfully by rose growers in the northern climates.

Gardening Skill

Doing the Minnesota Tip

You must protect rose plants against the ravages of winter if you wish them to survive. We are speaking of the hybrid teas, floribundas, grandifloras, miniatures, tree roses, and climbers. All of these must be well protected for winter. The shrub roses and many of the old garden roses do not need protection other than a mulch of leaves around them.

1. Soak the soil well the day before you are going to start tipping. Then dig a shallow trench up to the base of the plant, digging it carefully so as not to injure the bush or its roots. The trench should be about six inches deep and wide enough and long enough to accommodate the plant or plants, for more than one bush can be put in a trench.

2. With a spading fork, loosen the soil all around the bush. (Never use a spade for this loosening process, for you can cut the roots and severely damage the plant.) Move the fork gently back and forth in the soil around the plant, until the roots seem somewhat loosened. Then use the spading fork for leverave to push the plant into the trench. Wire hoops (made from coat hangers) may be used to hold the bush down until you cover it with several inches of soil.

3. Pack the soil in and around the canes so that you don't leave any air pockets. This is important. If you leave air pockets, that portion of the cane will die. Be sure to wear heavy gloves when packing the soil around the canes; those thorns can hurt.

4. After you have all your rose plants tipped and covered with soil, you may wait until the first week of November (depending on weather forecasts) to put leaves on the bed to a depth of about 1½ feet.

Common Questions About Roses

Dorothy Campbell

Asking questions about how to grow roses is almost harder than answering them. To prune or not to prune, tip or not to tip, dust or spray, pick or let perish, potted vs. bare root, and so on. It's hard to know what to ask. It's hard to know whom to ask — there's always that noted authority, your neighbor. Some people are so put off by the mystique of rose-growing, they never give it a chance.

It can get confusing, especially in the spring, the time of the fastest growth and development of rose plants. They go from bare stems and canes to fully leafed-out and budding plants in one month. The variety of the tasks, more than their difficulty, often confuses the new as well as the not-so-new grower. It's mostly a question of what to do and when to do it. I'll make it easy. I'll ask the questions ... and answer them, too.

How do I select a site for a rose garden? Perhaps the first consideration in selecting a site is that it be in an area you can see from some favorite place in your home. To be able to look out at your roses on a dreary, rainy day does wonders for the morale.

Pick a spot where your roses will have a good, if not beautiful, background. If you aren't fortunate enough to have a suitable natural setting, provide it or improvise one. Your roses are the jewels of your garden; provide the right setting for them.

Providing a background for a rose bed need not be expensive. Many attractive and fairly inexpensive fencings are available which would work beautifully and serve a double purpose by providing a place for climbing roses or clematis. Many varieties of attractive shrubs (including the lovely shrub roses) would create a lovely setting. Evergreens set off roses beautifully but should not be too close to the rose bed.

It has been said that roses need a place in the sun and a place on dry land. In other words, they want direct sunlight for at least half a day and a spot with good drainage. Roses also need to be out of reach of tree roots and where air circulates freely. These are elementary requirements. Roses can be planted in foundation plantings or perennial borders if these requirements are met, but the care of roses is much easier and their beauty is enhanced if they are grouped together and not scattered here and there.

If the area is very open, roses can be placed along the edge of the lawn, but avoid the rigid formality of straight lines; give a curving effect. Simplicity in planning is desirable. Numerous small beds cut in a lawn will look fussy and make for more work because of the time necessary for trimming around them. They are less effective for color grouping also.

Avoid a narrow place, such as between two houses, for the wind will tunnel through. Houses also cut off sun, and disease is a greater problem in a hemmed-in area. Too near a dense hedge or brick wall is bad; these absorb too much moisture.

Avoid low-lying areas; they often form natural frost pockets. Late frosts can play havoc with new growth that comes after pruning, resulting in malformed flowers or reduced crop of bloom. Beds in low-lying parts of a garden will be more subject to flooding and waterlogging of soil after heavy rains. Don't make your bed too wide. Six feet is a good width with which to work.

I can only have one rose bed. How should I place the colors? In years past, planting a rose garden with color harmony in mind was no problem. There were white, yellow, pink, and soft red roses, and all the colors, like well-behaved children, got along very nicely together. In the last 25 years, however, hybridizers have gone all out and have come up with hues and shades that Mother Nature never dreamed possible. It takes much thought and careful planning to plant the unique, spectacular colors in a rose bed and create a pleasing effect, showing off their dazzling beauty and not "killing" the soft pinks and deep reds.

If you have room for just one rose bed, plan carefully before you plant your roses. Keep the vibrant, fluorescent oranges and orange-reds at one end, judiciously separated by as much distance as possible from the soft pinks and velvety reds. In between, plant the yellows and yellow blends, the bicolors, then the whites at about the center of the bed. Then go on with the delicate pastels, the lovely pinks and pink blends, the rosy shades, and finally, the deep, glowing reds. By staggering the rows of roses (not placing a plant directly behind the rose bush in the adjoining row), you can get more roses in a given area, and the effect will be more pleasing.

Is May too late to start a new rose bed? Definitely not, but you will have to plant potted rose bushes. Bare root plants must be planted by May 15; after that the weather is usually too warm. By the time you have prepared the new rose bed, it will probably be too late to set out bare root bushes.

In starting a new rose bed, prepare the ground thoroughly. Work plenty of organic material into the soil, and let it settle well (at least 10 days or more) before planting. Space the bushes at least 2-1/2 feet apart, so there is good air circulation. Avoid overcrowding.

I've tried roses in the past and failed. What was I doing wrong? Buy potted plants from a reliable nursery. Don't buy "bargain" potted plants: the chances are great that they will have their roots jammed or curled into the pot. These roots will never be able to grow and develop, for they can't straighten themselves out. The plants will never amount to anything and probably won't even survive the first summer.

After purchasing the potted plants from a reliable nursery, let them acclimate to outside temperatures before putting them in the rose bed. These plants have been grown in a greenhouse or protected area, so they must be given time to adjust to outdoor living. They can be fertilized the same as established plants.

I've heard that roses are very heavy feeders. Is this true? Roses are reputed to be heavy feeders. Recommendations found in books often call for heavy (as much as one cup) applications of chemical fertilizers, applied usually twice during the growing season. It would be much better to substitute "steady" for "heavy". Rose plants respond much more to light applications of fertilizer applied more frequently. A heavy feeding (such as one cup) could very easily burn developing feeder roots which are close to the surface. So forget the "heavy" feeding; stick to the "steady," light feeding applied regularly and more often.

When should I feed my roses and with what? The first step in determining your feeding program is to have your soil tested. Soil samples can be tested at most county extension service offices; contact your local county agricultural agent. The report would give the levels of the major elements and the pH (whether the soil is acid or alkaline). Recommendations are made as to what is needed so that you could select the properly proportioned fertilizer (such as 8-16-16, 10-10-10, etc.).

Starting about the last week of April, work very generous amounts of organic matter into the soil (manure, compost, blends of various meals such as cottonseed, alfalfa, blood, bone and others, processed sludge, etc.). You can never have too much organic matter in the garden, and it is constantly being used up. Then about the first of every month from May until August, give a feeding of the granular or liquid fertilizer recommended for your soil.

At mid-month, extra treats may be given to your roses, but make this an organic food, such as liquid manure or diluted fish emulsion. Rose plants really respond to these extra organic feedings. Once a year, in the spring, chelated iron may be given your plants for better color. Follow directions as to amount.

What about roses planted this year? Newly planted bare root roses should not be given any inorganic fertilizer until after the first blooming period. Feed them the last week of June or first week of July with a well-balanced fertilizer and again early in August. They may be given the organic feedings along with the established rose plants.

When should I begin to spray the roses? Roses should be given a thorough spraying or dusting as soon as the plants are uncovered. Then in May, when the plants are leafing out (usually by the third week), start a regular spray or dusting schedule. Do it every 10 days until the middle of June. Then growth is very rapid, so spray or dust every week. It only takes a few minutes once a week to keep your roses healthy.

What type of mulch should I use? Wait until the soil has warmed thoroughly (usually the last of May or early June) before applying a mulch. The best type to use is one that breaks down reasonably fast and, in so doing, enriches the soil. Well-rotted manure or compost is best. Rotted sawdust works well, but if it continues to decay, additional nitrogen will be needed. Shredded oak leaves are fine, but not soft leaves, such as maple or birch; they compact too much. Pine needles are good.

Peat moss is attractive, but it has a disadvantage; it will get compacted, form a crust, and shed moisture. It needs to be stirred up often. Koko bean hulls are good but expensive. Buckwheat hulls have a tendency to mold, so must be stirred up also. Lawn clippings can be used, but put them on in very thin layers and allow to dry before adding more; otherwise they will get moldy and heat up. Never use clippings from a weedy lawn or one that has been treated with a weed killer.

Low-Maintenance Roses

Terry Schwartz

Imagine a tattered and torn Crusader of the 12th century stopping on his way back home to enjoy a flower that had not been seen in the European landscape since the decline of the Roman empire. Having never seen such beauty anywhere before, it is not hard to see why the Crusaders brought these shrub roses back into Europe and the gardens of noblemen and rich merchants. Once again roses became a part of the economy as well as the culture, grown for their perfumes and medicinal properties as well as their beauty.

Sometimes referred to today as "classic roses," gardeners are just beginning to pay attention to these older roses. Until recently they suffered from a lack of availability as well as a lack of information. Mention hardy roses and someone would say, "Oh, my mom had one of those," or "No thanks, I like to plant a variety of roses."

Well let me tell you, your mom didn't have one of these, and today there are enough varieties available that the average homeowner couldn't begin to plant them all in his or her yard.

Like to know more about them? Stick with me and I'll take you into a world of roses that most people don't even know exists.

Care

If you are like me, low-input gardening with great results is the way to go, and shrub roses really fit the bill. There's no making like a gopher and digging up all your plants and burying them at the first sign of frost, as you have to with the less-hardy hybrid teas. Secondly, a Ph.D. in chemistry isn't necessary to keep bugs off and diseases at bay. Also, hardy roses don't have the finicky water requirements of the hybrid teas. In fact, sometimes a little water stress will produce a better flush of blooms.

Another plus for the hardy types is that most all of them are grown on their own roots, not grafted onto other rootstocks. This means that if they should freeze to the ground, they will come back true to name, often fuller and richer than they were before. These roses will give you years of enjoyment with little or no care or replacement costs.

Background

Many people still refer to all of these roses as rugosa roses. The term hardy roses was coined because many of today's varieties have no rugosa blood in them at all. Frequently called "old-fashioned roses," these plants are far from being old. Some of the parent lines of these newer roses come from such varieties as *Rosa x kordesii*, which was used extensively by Herr Kordes in Germany during the 1950s. It was a variety that he never introduced, but used only for breeding purposes. Seedlings from this rose are very disease resistant. Many of the varieties from the Ottawa Research Station in Ontario have this parentage in them — 'Champlain', 'John Cabot', 'William Baffin', and 'Henry Kelsey' just to mention a few (more about these later).

This is not to say that the rugosa rose is no longer used. There has been much work done with it to develop some fine new varieties, such as 'Charles Albanel'. There are also some fine varieties that have been around for a while with Rugosa blood in them — varieties such as 'F.J. Grootendorst', a beautiful double red, 'Pink Grootendorst', and 'Hansa', a reddish purple rose, just to name a few. 'Agnes', a showy, double yellow also comes to mind. *Rosa arkansana*, a native of North America, is a low-growing compact shrub rose that has also lent itself to creating better varieties for the homeowner.

I could go on and bore you with all the crosses it took to get to these plants, but I'd rather tell you what they will look like in your own yard. So let's go on to look at some of these new — as well as some of the older —varieties of hardy roses.

Suggested Varieties

Cuthbert Grant. Luxuriant is the word that best describes the glossy, dark green foliage which sets off the dark red blossoms. Borne in clusters of three to six, each flower reaches up to four inches wide. This three-foot shrub is an outstanding introduction from Canada, where it was the Manitoba Centennial Rose. It is one of two favorites from the Parkland Series, developed by the Morden Research Station.

Morden Centennial. Like other Parkland varieties, this rose flowers on new wood and will flower freely even after being cut back severely. This is a floriferous shrub reaching three to four feet in height. The pink, mildly-scented flowers are borne either singly or in clusters of up to 15. It also has excellent disease resistance, being free of blackspot, rust and mildew.

Nearly Wild. This rose has got to be the leader in bloom, size, and disease resistance. It was introduced in 1941 but is now just starting to catch on. This is a mound-shaped plant resembling a wild rose, with beautiful, pink flowers that cover the plant all summer. The foliage is light green. When planted in mass plantings the fragrance can be incredible.

Assiniboine. Named for the famous garden in Winnipeg, this is not a rose to be overlooked. Its beautiful red flowers with creamy yellow centers make it a knockout in the home landscape. The plant itself reaches a comfortable four feet in height and in width. Its semi-double, three-inch flowers really put on a show when it's at peak bloom.

No need to worry about hardiness with this introduction from Canada. Established plants will bloom freely, even when they have been cut or killed back all the way to the ground. In fact, 'Assiniboine' has proven itself so well, that other varieties such as 'Morden Ruby' and 'Morden Amorette' have been bred from it. Both were introduced in 1977 and are superior in some respects. They are not as readily available, but worth mentioning should you ever run across them.

Morden Ruby. This introduction resembles a floribunda type of rose and has flowers that are ruby red, fully double and borne in clusters that start in June and continue until frost. It is quite resistant to mildew and rust and is moderately resistant to blackspot.

Morden Amorette. This rose blooms throughout the growing season, displaying carmine- to rose-colored flowers. It is relatively free from mildew and rust problems; however, blackspot can be a problem.

Adelaide Hoodless. This cross between *Rosa fireking* and *Rosa arkansana* is another Morden Station development. The slightly fragrant flowers are semi-double, bright red and measure 2-1/2 inches across. The glossy, green foliage of this shrub makes the flowers stand out even more. Other advantages include its resistance to blackspot and mildew and the fact that blooms appear from June until frost.

The Hunter. This is a rugosa hybrid from England with beautiful, double, bright red flowers that are very fragrant. It stays very compact and reaches only four feet in height. The foliage, which stays very clean, is dark green and again adds a lot to the flower color. It has recurrent bloom throughout the season and, in my opinion, the flower equals any floribunda.

Therese Bugnet. This rugosa type from Canada has a lot of great features going for it. Its flowers are large and pink and borne on shoots that can carry up to 12 buds. The plant does not sucker and blooms from mid-June until frost.

Hansa is a charming variety that makes a beautiful flowering hedge or showy plant. (MSHS)

Hansa. While certainly not new, this variety is not commonly known among today's younger gardeners. It has a reddish-purple flower that has a very pleasing scent and blooms throughout the summer. One other nice thing

about this plant is that the large red hips remain after the petals fall, adding interest in fall and winter.

Charles Albanel. This extremely hardy rugosa type comes to us from the Ottawa Research Station in Canada. It was introduced in 1982. A low-growing plant, reaching heights of only 12 to 15 inches, it makes a gorgeous ground cover. It flowers freely in early summer and then sporadically throughout the remainder of the season. It has been tested in Ottawa since 1972 and other locations in Canada and the northern United States since 1980, and has survived winters in these areas with no winterkill.

Champlain. Another of the newer hardy roses to be developed, I think the flower color of 'Champlain' ranks with the best. Although it is usually referred to as red, I think crimson is much more descriptive. It flowers freely all summer long, and is resistant to both blackspot and mildew. The slightly fragrant flowers reach 2 to 2-1/2 inches across. This is a low-growing plant, reaching a height of about three feet, making it suitable for smaller spaces.

Agnes. Lack of space allows me to describe only this one yellow rose, but I consider it to be one of the best. It has all of the qualities people look for in a rose. It was developed in Canada in 1922 from a cross between *R. rugosa* and *R. foetida*. It will grow almost anywhere with a minimal amount of coddling. It looks good both as a specimen and in mass plantings. The highly scented double flowers, which open yellow and then fade to white, appear in full force in early summer and then continue to appear intermittently throughout the summer. The foliage is somewhat crinkled. The plant itself will grow four to six feet tall. Other yellow varieties include 'Father Hugo', 'Harrison's Yellow', 'Primrose', and 'Persian Yellow'. The flowers of 'Father Hugo' and 'Primrose' are single, while the other two have double flowers.

"Persian Yellow" is a profuse bloomer with double, well-formed flowers. Plant where color is needed. (MSHS)

William Baffin. In the world of hardy roses, 'William Baffin' is considered a climber. Like other climbing roses, it does not have tendrils and will require tying to a fence or trellis. It does not require any pruning and is hardy enough to allow the branches to remain on the fence or trellis throughout the winter. This is a real asset for those of us who want a climbing rose, but don't want to fight with 15 feet of thorns every fall. The mildly fragrant pink flowers are borne in clusters of up to 30. The plant is highly resistant to blackspot and mildew. Unfortunately, this variety is not widely available at this time, but it is worth mentioning for those of you who are lucky enough to spot it in some obscure catalog.

These varieties only begin to hint at what is available in hardy roses, but as you can see, it's a whole new world — and a brave one, at that, especially when it comes to winters in the northland.

THE NORTHERN GARDENER'S LIBRARY

Chapter 6

Appendices

Mail Order Sources

Zone Hardiness Map

About the Authors

Mail Order Sources

NAME OF COMPANY	TYPE OF MERCHANDISE	REMARKS
Stokes Seeds, Inc. Box 548 Buffalo, NY 14240	All kinds of seeds; good selection	Good all around source, excellent cultural advice, excellent source of vegetable seeds
Park Seed Co. Cokesbury Rd. Greenwood, SC 29647	All kinds of seeds, good selection, unusual garden perennials	Good all around source, excellent cultural advice, house plant seeds
Harris Seeds 961 Lyell Ave. Rochester, NY 14606	All kinds of seeds	Very reliable, good source for vegetables
Thompson & Morgan P.O. Box 1308 Jackson, NJ 08527	All kinds of seeds	Good source with an English flare
Farmer Seed & Nursery Faribault, MN 55021	All kinds of seeds & nursery stock	Local source, very reliable
Antonelli Brothers 2545 Capitola Rd. Santa Cruz, CA 95062	Tuberous begonia seed, tuberous begonias & gloxinia	Very reliable
Gardener's Supply 128 Intervale Rd. Burlington, VT 05401	Innovative garden equipment & gadgets	Very reliable
Van Ness Water Gardens 2460 N. Euclid Ave. Upland, CA 91786	Water lilies, bog plants, pond equipment	Excellent catalog
Burpee & Co. Warminister, PA 18974	Seeds, bulbs, plants, nursery stock	Very reliable
Heritage Gardens 1 Meadow Ridge Rd., Shenandoah, IA 51601	Garden perennials, vines, fruit trees, shrubs, shade trees	Reliable local source
Busse Gardens Rt. 2, Box 238 Cokato, MN 55321	Good variety of garden perennials	Good local source for all perennials
Ambergate Gardens 8015 Krey Ave. Waconia, MN 55387	Unusual garden perennials, Martagon lilies	Good local source for garden perennials
Borbeleta Gardens 15974 Canby Ave. Faribault, MN 55021	Daylilies, lilies, irises daffodils, Siberian irises	Good local source with excellent catalog

NAME OF COMPANY	TYPE OF MERCHANDISE	REMARKS
Van Bourgondien P.O. Box A 245 Farmindale Rd., Rt. 109 Babylon, NY 11702	Seasonal bulbs	Good source
Epicure Seeds Ltd. P.O. Box 450 Brewster, NY 10509	Unusual vegetables	European flare
Johnny's Selected Seeds Albion, ME 04910	Vegetable specialist	Good catalog with excellent cultural instructions
L. L. Olds Seed Co. P.O. Box 7790 2901 Packers Ave. Madison, WI 53707-7790	All seeds plus nursery stock	Good local source
Vermont Bean Seed Co. Garden Lane, Bomoseen VT 05732	Vegetable specialist	Good source, very unusual
Gurney's Seed & Nursery Co. 110 Capital St. Yankton, SD 57079	All kinds of seeds & nursery stock	Good source
Earl May Seed & Nursery Shenandoah, IA 51603	Seed & nursery stock	Good local source
Jung Seed Co. Randolph, WI 53956	Seeds, house plants, garden perennials	Good local source
North Star Gardens 19060 Manning Tr. Marine, MN 55047	Raspberry & blueberry specialist	Aimed at the market grower, good catalog
Jordan Seeds 6400 Upper Afton Rd. Woodbury, MN 55125	Vegetable seeds, market growers supplies	Aimed at the market gardener
Wilson Bros, Floral Co. Roachdale, IN 46172	Geranium specialist, African violets, fuchsia, begonias, house plants	Very reliable, good source
Donahue's Gardens P.O. Box366 420 S. W. 10th St. Faribault, MN 55021	Minnesota garden chrysan-themums, clematis, begonias, assorted hanging material	Excellent source for garden mums, local source with good quality
Prairie Restorations, Inc. P.O. Box 327 Princeton, MN 55371	Seeds for MN native prairie grasses & wild flowers	MN genotypes, locally grown

USDA Plant Hardiness Zone Map

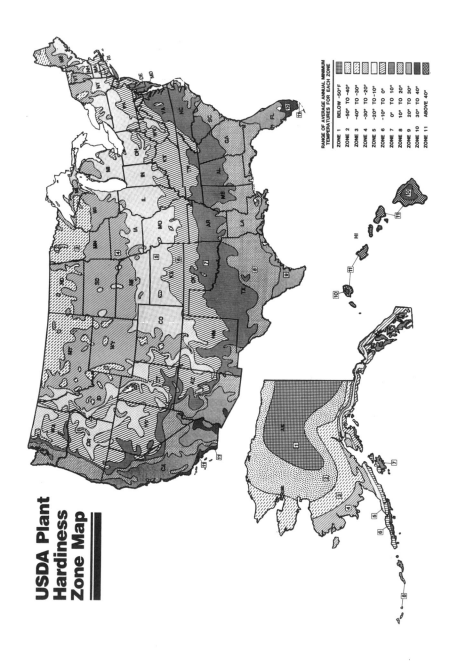

RANGE OF AVERAGE ANNUAL MINIMUM TEMPERATURES FOR EACH ZONE

ZONE 1   BELOW -50°F
ZONE 2   -50° TO -40°
ZONE 3   -40° TO -30°
ZONE 4   -30° TO -20°
ZONE 5   -20° TO -10°
ZONE 6   -10° TO 0°
ZONE 7   0° TO 10°
ZONE 8   10° TO 20°
ZONE 9   20° TO 30°
ZONE 10 30° TO 40°
ZONE 11 ABOVE 40°

About the Authors

Fred Glasoe is a regular contributor to *Minnesota Horticulturist*, as well as the host of a weekly radio program on gardening. An avid promoter of gardening in the Twin Cities, he spends as much time as he can in his own back yard.

Glenn Ray was executive secretary of the Minnesota State Horticultural Society (MSHS) for several years and maintains a "perennial masterpiece" in Minnetonka, Minnesota.

Ainie Busse is a member of the Wright County Chapter of MSHS. She owns a perennial nursery and is a frequent speaker on flower gardening.

Charlie King lives and gardens in Bloomington and is a regular contributor to *Minnesota Horticulturist*.

Michael Heger is the owner of Ambergate Gardens, a nursery specializing in perennial plants, in Waconia, Minnesota.

Reverend Lawrence Rule, now that he's retired, tests All-America Selections for Zone 3 at his garden in Brainerd, Minnesota.

Esther Filson is a Master Gardener who grows and arranges floral materials in Cottage Grove, Minnesota.

Dorothy Campbell is a member of the Minnesota Rose Society and wrote regularly for *Minnesota Horticulturist* on roses.

Terry Schwartz, a native of northern Minnesota, now lives in Cottage Grove, where he is a professional nurseryman.

Betty Ann Mech owns Rice Creek Gardens in Blaine, MN.

Deborah Brown, St. Paul, coordinates horticultural resources to answer questions from the public as director for the U of M Extension Service Dial-U Clinic. She also speaks and writes about gardening in Minnesota.